Media Reporting

Principles and Practices of Modern Journalism in a Multimedia World

James Glen Stovall

Tennessee Journalism Series

First Inning Press

in conjunction with the

Intercollegiate Online News Network

Table of Contents

Forward

Nobody with a living brain cell goes into the newspaper business for the money. They're in it because digging up the truth is interesting and consequential work, and for sheer entertainment it beats the hell out of humping products for GE or Microsoft. Done well, journalism brings to light chicanery, oppression and injustice, though such concerns seldom weigh heavily on those who own newspapers.

-- Carl Hiassen is a reporter and columnist for the *Miami Herald*. He is also a novelist, and his books include *Tourist Season* and *Double Whammy*.

Central to the act of journalism is the act of reporting. Journalism cannot exist without reporting, without reporters who are willing to dig up information in all sorts of unlikely places and from all sorts of unlikely people. Nothing matters in journalism without reporting.

That's why this book was written. Students who have an interest in journalism should -- must -- understand that good reporting is the core. Intelligent, insightful, efficient gathering of information. Information that is original, relevant, important and useful.

Journalism doesn't exist without it.

Reporting is hard work. It is frustrating and difficult. Reporters are constantly called upon to use their wit and imagination, to think of where information is and who has it -- and then to persuade those who have it to give it up. Reporters do not have subpoena power. They cannot compel sources to part with their information.

So a reporter must sell the source on the importance of what the reporter is doing.

None of that is easy.

But reporting, hard as it is, can also be fun and exciting. It can take a young person to places he or she would never see otherwise. It can put the reporter in touch with the most interesting people on earth. It gives the reporter a front-row seat on the human condition.

It's not always a pretty picture, but it is almost inevitably interesting and enlightening.

Media Reporting: Principles and Practices of Journalism in a Multimedia World will give you some of the basic concepts of what a reporter does and how a reporter goes about the business of journalism.

***

The author and the Tennessee Journalism Series would like to thank the folks at the **Joan Schorenstein Center on the Press, Politics and Public Policy** for permission to use the statistical terms sidebar on page 81 and the campus reporting ideas on page 117.

Contributors to this book

Edward Caudill, a professor of journalism at the University of Tennessee, whose teaching specialties are history and reporting. He is the author of a number of books. More information: http://jem.cci.utk.edu/users/ed-caudill

Melanie Faizer, a lecturer in journalism at UT, who worked as a multimedia reporter, editor and television producer at Bloomberg News, a financial news company, in New Jersey, New York City and London, England. More information: http://jem.cci.utk.edu/users/melanie-faizer-0

Maria Fontenot, a lecturer in journalism at UT, who has extensive experience in broadcast news.

Nicholas Geidner, an assistant professor of journalism at UT, who has extensive experience in broadcast and web production. More information: http://jem.cci.utk.edu/users/nicholas-geidner

Mark Harmon, a professor of journalism at UT, who has written two books and has worked as a TV news producer, radio reporter, and host of a radio news interview program. More information: http://jem.cci.utk.edu/users/mark-harmon

Mike Martinez, an assistant professor of journalism at UT, who spent his professional career expanding a palette of journalistic skills at four newspapers and a wire service. More information: http://jem.cci.utk.edu/users/michael-t-martinez

Amber Roessner, an assistant professor of journalism at UT, whose professional experience includes a stint as an award-winning sports reporter. She teaches history and reporting at UT. More information: http://jem.cci.utk.edu/users/amber-roessner

Author
James Glen Stovall has taught journalism at UT since 2006. Previously he taught at the University of Alabama and Emory and Henry College. He is the author of numerous books, including *Writing for the Mass Media*. More information: http://jem.cci.utk.edu/users/james-glen-stovall

Tennessee Journalism Series

This book is a part of the **Tennessee Journalism Series**.

The Tennessee Journalism Series is a set of texts and instructional material developed by the faculty of the University of Tennessee School of Journalism and Electronic Media for journalism instructors around the world.

The idea behind the series is "multimedia first."

That is, these books are built for the iPad and contain a variety of multimedia elements: text, audio, video, photo galleries, interactive images, and interactive reviews and quizzes.

At present, six books are available on the iBookstore for downloading to an iPad:

• **Introduction to Journalism**

• **Reporting: An Introduction**

• **Photojournalism**

• **The First Amendment**

• **Feature Writing**

• **Media Reporting**

Other books under development include texts on sports journalism, audio journalism and video journalism. Various aspects of the history of journalism will also be part of this series.

1. Journalistic reporting

Journalists gather information, but they do so in particular ways and for particular purposes. This chapter explores some of the basic aspects of being a reporter.

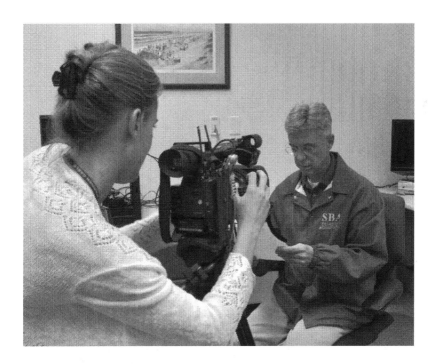

1.1 Information

Purpose of this section

To understand that gathering information is the first and most important job of the journalist.

To develop an idea of what kind of information is of interest to the journalist and of significance to an audience.

Importance

Gathering information is the most important part of the journalist's job. Information consists of facts, opinions, ideas, assertions and interpretations that ultimately will help the news consumer understand the part of the world to which the journalism is directed.

Journalism begins with information. Gathering information is the first job of the journalist.

That information must meet certain conditions.

Most importantly, it must be factual and accurate. Journalists seek information that is factual – events that actually happened, what people really said and did, how people really feel. They try to sort out the actual from the fantasy – that is, what people think or hope or wish had happened from what actually happened.

Obtaining and disseminating accurate information is the chief goal of journalists. Much of the process that journalists use to gather information is mean to ensure the accuracy of the information they have.

Accuracy is a concept that will come up again and again as we discuss what it means to be a journalist. Journalists fear inaccurate information because it means that they have failed at their job.

Another condition of the information that journalists gather is that it be significant. Significant means that it should be important to a sizable number of people. The fact that your pet (dog, cat, rabbit, whatever) is sick is important to you and your family, but it is not meaningful to those outside your immediate circle.

If your pet is being affected by a condition that is affecting many other pets, however, that information is significant, and it is something that a journalist might be interested in.

Closely associated with significance is the condition that the information should be interesting to some portion of the audience. Not everything that appears in the news media is of interest to everyone, of course. The comings and goings of many celebrities are of absolutely no interest or importance to many, many people. Yet, we will hear about them because there are a significant number of people (you, perhaps) who want to know this information.

Judging how interesting information is to an audience is tricky business for journalists. They must often go beyond their personal interests and inclinations and be aware that there are many people who expect the news media to provide information about a wide range of topics. Sports is a case in point. Many people care nothing for sports and will never read a sports story or listen to a sports broadcast. Yet, obviously, sports gets major attention from the news media because there are enough people who are interested in it to make a difference to news organizations. And there are enough people who are not only interested but deeply interested for sports to be a major part of the news media's offerings.

Journalists should develop a wide range of interests, but they should also recognize the audience's interests range far more widely than their personal interests.

Yet another condition of the information a journalist gathers is that it be current information. In fact, it should be the most up-to-date information that is available about an event or topic.

This factor of the timeliness of the information is terribly important for news organizations and for the journalists themselves. It is an important part of modern journalism that information be the latest, most up-to-date information that can be obtained.

And by up-to-date, what we really mean is up-to-the minute.

Old news is not news, as journalists like to say; it's history. What happened last week is not nearly as interesting to the journalist as what happened yesterday. And what happened yesterday is not as interesting as what happened in the last hour or the last give minutes.

That is one of the things that makes journalism so difficult. Journalists are in a constant race to shorten the amount of time between obtaining and disseminating information, and that is especially as the web as become a major medium of journalism. The web is always on and always available. Audiences expect the web to be consistently and constantly updated with new information.

In class

A. Discuss the ways in which you get information on things that you are interested in. Do you find that you always start – or think about starting – with the same sources?

B. How do you get information on the things you are planning to buy?

Ask yourself

A. How good are you at getting information? Journalists have to develop special skills at knowing where information is located so they can use their time efficiently. How would you find the following information quickly?

Famous people who were born on September 8.

The weather forecast for next week.

Requirements for admission to your major state university.

The top-grossing movies from the previous weekend.

B. Select a news story about a significant current event. Print that story out, and beside it list all of the facts about the event or subject. (Just make it a short checklist; you don't have to use complete sentences.)

The **Tennessee Journalism Series** includes an Introduction to Journalism (below) that may be of interest to you. Check it out on the iBookstore here:

https://itunes.apple.com/us/book/introduction-to-journalism/id532576726?ls=1

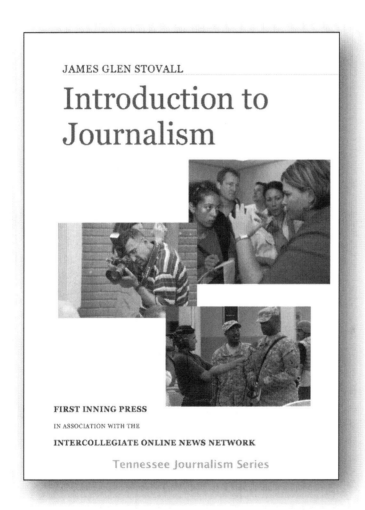

1.2 Accuracy

Purpose of this section
To impress upon students the all-important goal of journalism is to obtain and present accurate information.

Importance
Accuracy is the number one goal of the journalist. Many of the standard procedures of newsgathering have been developed to ensure this goal is met.

The first commandment of modern journalism remains accuracy (though it wasn't always so). Present accurate information in an accurate context and in a way that can be understood by the reader, listener or viewer. That's the reporter's job.

What does that mean? How can a reporter make it happen?

Many errors, if not most, are made at the reporting stage of the journalistic process. A good and careful reporter is the best defense against inaccuracy. But both reporters and editors have to take responsibility for all the errors in their publication, and they need to systematically guard against making errors.

So, how?

• Presenting information that is verifiable. (See the section on verification.) Some information should not be produced by professional journalistic organizations because it cannot be checked. We used to put most rumors in that category, although the standard here may be changing.

• Making sure interpretations of information are fair and reasonable and that they are stronger than other interpretations.

• Gathering information from various sources that might confirm the information we have or give us additional perspective on it. The reporter must exercise careful judgment in weighing the credibility of those sources.

Many times in the reporting and editing of news stories, the nature of the information points to one and only one source, so this last procedure may not be possible. Reporters and editors must be practiced and knowledgeable enough to discern that – all of which argues for a wide range of knowledge on the part of a journalist. It also argues for journalists being specialists in something – that is, having an intimate knowledge of some subject.

What are you a specialist in? What do you know more about than anyone else in the room? (Instructors: Ask this question of your students and you'll get some interesting answers.)

Achieving accuracy

What are the practical steps we can take as journalists to achieve accuracy? Here are a few:

• **question, question, question.** Raise questions about every sentence you read. Does this sound right? Does it pass a smell test? Could the source have really said this? Does this make sense? Do I know something different? If you do, it's your responsibility to change the copy or to raise a question with the instructor.

• **check what you can check.** The stylebook and dictionary are the first places to begin. If an article refers to the "assassination of President John Kennedy in 1964," check it out (it's wrong!). As time allows, check anything you think there will be a record of.

• **names, dates, times.** Names of people in news stories should always be checked for spelling and appropriate titles. Go back to the reporter (or ask the instructor) for a check on dates and times.

• **do the math.** When a story contains numbers, make sure you add them up. If a story says something like "35 years ago in 1969," make sure that 1969 is 35 years ago (it isn't).

• **internal logic.** Reporters contradict themselves in their writing; it happens more than you might think. Stay sensitive to finding these contradictions. Sometimes there is a reason for including contradictory information, but those reasons should be obvious or spelled out for the reader. The editor has to deal with them.

• **use the language literally.** A reporter wrote that that the city council reacted "violently" to the mayor's budget proposal. Yet, there was no fighting during the city council meeting. Everything was civil; no violence at all. The word "violently" was used inaccurately, making the description of the event inaccurate.

In journalism, we speak literally, not figuratively, and we deal with specific, concrete information rather than vague ideas.

• **use your common sense.** You don't enter a parallel universe when you are an editor; you deal with a very real world. Words, phrases, sentences, statements and other items that sound out of kilter probably are. Deal with them; fix them. Make them make sense.

Judging the accuracy of a piece of writing and correcting the writing to make it accurate is not unlike what we do as adults in reacting to the world around us. We have to decide what is true, relevant and accurate in order to make good decisions about our lives. In journalistic editing, those processes are the same – only they are often done with more intensity, with the knowledge that decisions will affect the lives of others, and with the pressure of a deadline.

An additional note: John Early McIntyre, assistant managing editor for the copydesk at the *Baltimore Sun,* has an excellent piece on the Poynter web site about the importance of editing. In it, he cites a 2003 conference on Editing for the Future held at the First Amendment Center in Nashville. The web site for the conference contains many resources for those interested in editing, including a session devoted to accuracy. That session was led by Margaret Holt, customer service editor of the *Chicago Tribune.* During her presentation, she told the story of the time when the Tribune got serious about guarding against inaccuracies:

Since 1992 the *Chicago Tribune* has hired a proofreader to do an errors-per-page annual report, so the newsroom can track errors from year to year. "We were abysmal starting out," she said. "I think we were as high as 4.82 errors per page."

However, the *Tribune's* accuracy program kicked into high gear in 1995 when it suffered an accuracy "meltdown." A senior writer misidentified a top *Tribune* executive in an obituary of a beloved editor. That executive was "not happy," Holt said. The obit was published on a Saturday, and by Monday, the executive ordered the *Tribune* to establish an error policy.

In class

A. Select a recent major news event that would be covered by reporters from all of the major news organizations – a natural disaster, for instance. Read carefully the reports from at least three of these news organizations. Do any of these reports have facts that are conflicting?

B. If a friend called you and said a SWAT team had gathered around a house down the street and was about to charge, would you believe him or her? How would you find out if he or she was accurate?

Ask yourself

Why is accuracy so important to journalists? List all of the reasons you can think of – even those not necessarily included in the text of this module.

1.3 Verification

Purpose of this section
Journalism distinguishes itself from other writing with a strict process of verification.

Importance
Journalists learn how to attribute their information to the sources from which that information is taken. They do this seamlessly in their writing.

Vital to the process of verification is being able to think logically, analytically and skeptically.

Journalism distinguishes itself from other writing through the concept of verification. The "discipline of verification," a term coined by Bill Kovich and Tom Rosentiel, authors of *The Elements of Journalism*, allows journalism to rise to the level of believability that few other forms of information presentation have.

So what is verification?

In short, it is making sure you are right in what you say. It is making sure you are accurate in every detail of what you write.

And why is it so important?

Journalists and news organizations consistently try to develop a reputation for credibility. They want what they say to be believed by the reader or listener, whether the news consumer agrees with it or not. News organizations can do this only by making extra and sometimes extraordinary efforts to verify the information they present to the consumer. Over time, consumers will come to trust the news outlets.

This all may sound logical and straightforward, and in many ways it is. If you develop a reputation for honesty among your friends, you will be believed when you tell them something.

But in the process of journalism – when reporters are working on several stories at once and facing daily deadline pressures – verifying information so that it rises to the standards of the profession may be difficult and ever-frustrating.

Every reporter develops ways to verify information efficiently, but there are some general principles and techniques that all reporters use.

First, all reporters verify basic information such as the spelling of names, the exact wording of titles, making sure direct quotations are exactly the words that were spoken, and other basic tenets. The verification usually is done by the reporter asking the source.

Yes, you should always ask a source how to spell his or her name. Always. It is not insulting or irritating to do so. Rather, it shows that you are trying to be careful. Misspelling someone's name is a serious error and WILL insult a source and demonstrate that you do not have the discipline to be a journalist.

You should also ask the source his or her job title if that is relevant to the story. In fact, any information that you plan to use about the source, you should verify with the source. And if you doubt what the source has told you, you should try to find that information from an independent source.

Vital to the process of verification is being able to think logically, analytically and skeptically.

Notice that in most straight news reports, most of the information in the report is attributed to some source. Attribution is a part of the writing style of the journalist, and we will say much more about it in the next section. There are ways to properly attribute information that do not intrude into the writing, and the journalist must learn these techniques.

In this section, however, our focus is on reporting and some of the ways that reporters verify information.

One common technique is one that we have already alluded to: finding the same information from two independent sources. If two people who haven't had contact with each other are telling you the same thing, chances are that information is more believable. Having multiple sources does not always ensure that the information is correct, but it is a step in the right direction.

Another technique is to evaluate the source of the information, not just the information itself. Does the source have some special knowledge? Is the source in a position to know the information that the reporter needs? Finding the best sources of information and judging the credibility of the source is one of the major jobs of the reporter, and we devote a whole module to these problems later in this section of *Reporting: An Introduction.*

Evaluating the information itself is a natural part of the verification process. How likely and logical is the information? Does what the source say make sense? Some reporters use the expression "smell test" for information. Does information pass the "smell test"; that is, does it seem right on its face or is there something amiss or askew that needs to be questioned or checked out?

Vital to this process is being able to think logically and analytically. Is one thing related to another? Is something caused by something else? A reporter is constantly putting information to these tests.

Another word for this is skepticism. Reporters are skeptical of what they read, hear and see. They are always on a quest to "check it out."

Also vital to this process is the accumulated knowledge that reporters carry in their heads. Reporters should know as much about as many things as possible. They should read widely. They should talk with interest to many people. They should learn to listen actively and ask questions that will elicit information from people. And they should try to keep information in their heads so that they can be more efficient in the process of verification.

(The process of knowledge accumulation begins early in life and becomes part of the intellectual make-up of reporters. If you have not begun this process in earnest, now is the time to start. Even if you don't consider yourself a particularly "good" student, you can make up you mind to gather as much information and remember as much of it as possible. You can, in fact, make yourself smart.)

In addition to a wide range of general knowledge, reporters develop specialties in topics that are of interest to them. These topics can include anything – music, sports, video games, cars, science, literature and poetry, or any number of other subjects. As a student, it's not too early think about what specialties you might want to develop. The decisions that you make at this point are not ones that you are stuck with. You can always change your mind and go on to other things that might catch your interest. The important thing is to start doing this now.

Finally, those reporters who work in traditional news organizations find that they have a partner in the process of verification. That partner is the editor (and sometimes several editors). Editors raise questions about the information the reporter has. They suggest ways information can be verified. They bring their accumulated knowledge and experience to the process. They set the standards of information verification for the next organization.

In class

Use this search term on a good search engine: "errors on Wikipedia." Read some of the entries that discuss the mistakes that are on Wikipedia. What does this say about the process of verification? How does this make you feel about using Wikipedia as a source for your reports and school assignments?

Ask yourself

Select a long news story in the *New York Times* or the *Washington Post* and read it carefully. Is there evidence within the story about how the reporter verified the information?

1.4 Sources

Purpose of this section
To give students an idea of the different types of sources of information and how journalists use them.

Importance
Beginning journalists need to understand where they can obtain information and the three types of sources – personal, stored and observational – that are available to them.

Newswriting depends on information. The quality of the writing is tied to the quality of the information. The quality of the information depends on its source.

Reporting is the basic activity of journalism. Good journalism depends almost entirely on good reporting -- having the latest, most accurate, most credible information. (Writing is also important and an integral part of reporting.) Newswriters must understand information and sources in order to present the information properly to the audience.

Journalists have three types of sources they can go to for information:

Stored sources. This refers to information you can look up, in a book, in a library, on the Web – anywhere that information is recorded. The good reporter knows sources of information and can find them quickly.

Once, this was considered the least useful of all types of sources for the journalist. The web has changed that, however. Now because of the web, stored information can be accessed quickly and readily, and that information is much more likely to be more recent. Even the web does not solve the basic problems of stored sources: They are static (they can't be questioned), and they still may not contain the very latest information.

Observational sources. This is information that you can get from personal experience, by going to a city council meeting, a fire, a press conference, etc.

Reporters like to be on the scene. They like to be at events. Covering news from afar is not always satisfactory. They like to see with their own eyes, hear with their own ears. They like to talk to the people who are there and get the sights and sounds and smells of a news event.

Being an eyewitness to something and being able to talk to people who have experienced it is an experience that cannot be duplicated. Reporters learn to prepare themselves to cover an event by:

• learning as much as they can about the event beforehand

• getting into a position to see and hear what is going on

• talking with people who are also experiencing the event

• taking good notes; using a digital recorder; making notes to themselves immediately after the event

• taking pictures

We will discuss being present at an event in more detail in the section about on-the-scene reporting.

Watch media trainer Dave Bloss as he talks about developing sources in this YouTube video

http://youtu.be/JEaUOp_nKEs (6:58).

Personal sources. This is information that you get from talking to people. Most news reporters have to interview people to complete their news stories.

Being able to talk to people -- and getting people to talk to them -- is one of the most important skills of reporters. Many people are reluctant to talk with reporters for fear of being misquoted or afraid of the consequences of being in the news. Others are eager to talk with reporters but they may not have good information or they may be pushing their own agenda or point of view.

Reporters must learn to get the most from their sources by:

• finding the right people to talk to (VERY IMPORTANT), rather than using "sources of convenience"

• respecting their feelings and position

• dealing with them ethically by identifying oneself as a reporter, understanding the principles of on-the-record and off-the-record conversations, and maintaining the confidentiality of sources even when it is difficult to do so (such as being faced with going to jail)

• learning how to interview people properly

Attribution

One of the conventions of news writing is that you give the reader some idea of what the source of the information is. This is called attribution. Three things you should know about attribution are:

• Most important information in a news story should be attributed to some source;

• Information that is well known does not need to be attributed; for instance, you would not write, "The lake is on the north side of town," the sheriff said;

• Sometimes the source of the information is so obvious that it does not need any direct attribution;

• Information that a reporter gathers from on-the-scene reporting generally is not attributed (unless it comes directly from another eyewitness), but it is written in such a way that the reader understands that the reporter was there to see the event.

News reporters want the best information available; therefore, they will try to gather it from the people who know the most or who are closest to a situation. Not only are these people likely to have the best information, but they are also likely to be the most credible sources.

In class

Select a news story about a recent event and see if you can identify the types of sources – personal, stored or observational – that the reporter used to get the various pieces of information for the story.

Ask yourself

Some people are uncomfortable doing what journalists have to do – call up people they do not know, identify themselves and persuade them to spend some time answering questions. How about you? Would you be comfortable doing that? Do you think you could develop enough confidence to do that regularly?

1.5 Credibility

Purpose of this section
To teach students that journalists judge the credibility of information based on the credibility of the sources of that information.

Importance
The world is filled with information, facts, pseudo-information, assertions and opinions. The job of the journalist is to filter this blizzard and find information that is true, useful and interesting.

This is truly the Information Age.

That term was prevalent before the advent of the World Wide Web in the early 1990s, and the web has made it even more appropriate for our times. Never has so much information been so readily available to so many people. And never have so many people been able to contribute to the pool of information that is within reach of the general population.

As individuals, we can submerse ourselves in information about the most esoteric topics. Select any search engine (Google, Yahoo, etc.) and any topic (baseball, beekeeping, books, etc.), and within seconds you will be overcome with so much information that you could spend the rest of your day sorting through it.

As individuals, we need help in sorting through the maze of conflicting facts, statements, assertions, advice, commands, intelligence, etc., so that we can understand what is important and useful for use and for our society.

Journalists are there to help us.

Journalists must not only gather information but must also develop ways to judge the credibility of the information they acquire. They do this by systematically judging the credibility of their sources. This is an ongoing process and intimately a part of the work of the reporter. In the previous section, we discussed how journalists acquire information and the types of sources they use. In this module, we will talk about judging credibility.

How do journalists know if something they read or hear is accurate and important?

Journalists try to find experts on the topic they are research. Lots of people may have opinions about a topic. Experts have facts and knowledge.

Experts are people who generally are acknowledged by their education or experience to have facts and knowledge about a topic. Experts are the people whose business it is to know about a topic. They may even be people who make their living by having this knowledge.

Problem: Let's say you had to find out the value of a Barbie doll manufactured in the late 1950s or early 1960s. How would you do that? Who would know? Whom would you call? Who would be the expert in something like that? Re-read the previous paragraph and see if that gives you a clue.

Experts on variety of topics can be found anywhere and everywhere. Journalists often look to colleges and universities and to government agencies to find experts because of the broad base of their interest and knowledge. People in these places are in the business of acquiring knowledge and information and applying that knowledge to situations or passing that knowledge on to others.

If you have a local college or university, you should look on the web site at the list of departments (English, biology, physics, business, etc.) within the institution. The faculty within each of these departments can be considered experts on many topics within the broad subject area of the department.

Another type of person that journalists go to for information because of their built-in credibility are officials. Officials are people who are in charge. They have titles and responsibilities, and the assumption is that they know more than people who are not in charge. For instance:

• a chief of police knows more about law enforcement than other people in the city or county;

• a president of the Parent-Teachers Association knows more about the fund-raising efforts of the PTA than anyone else;

• the director of the local orchestra knows more about the programs the orchestra will present this season than anyone else.

Because there are different levels that officials have within organizations, the top official may not always be the most credible person – the person with the best information – about a specific topic that the organization oversees. There may be some lower-ranking official who has more knowledge or experience about a certain area. In fact, reporters often learn that clerks and secretaries know more about what is going on than their bosses.

A third kind of person whom journalists may seek out in researching an article are persons who have an interest in the topic at hand. By that we mean not just people who are interested in something but those people whose lives, businesses, families or activities are affected by the topic. People who "have an interest" are likely to have information, experience and even expertise in a certain topic.

But because they have an interest, journalists must take care in using the information these people provide. Journalists must judge whether or not this interest has affected the amount of information people are willing to give or the interpretation they put on that information. In order to make this judgment, journalists must know what the interest is and how likely the sources are to let this interest affect their information.

In politics, this is called "spin," and the journalist must judge what kind of spin the source is putting on the information.

(This is the reason that many people, including possibly some of your teachers, do not Wikipedia.com to provide good information. The problem with Wikipedia is that you do not KNOW who is writing and editing the information. Consequently, you are unable to check to see if there is any "spin" that you should be aware of.)

As a part of the reporting process, journalists learn to listen carefully, evaluate information and sources, test that information against their own logic and insights, check the information with alternative sources and present the information to other journalists (editors) within their news organization. As they gain more reporting experience, they develop their own instincts, and they learn what sources are the most credible and which ones can be trusted, so that the process become more efficient.

In class

Take the problem mentioned in this text – the one concerning the Barbie doll – and try to solve it.

Ask yourself

Who is the person you would believe no matter what he or she told you? Why? List as many reasons as you can think of.

What news organizations or news web sites do you find most reliable? Which are the ones you might turn to if you want the day's news?

1.6 Professionalism

Purpose of this section
To lay out some of the ground rules under which journalists operate and to explain some of the reasons for and implications of these rules.

Importance
How a journalist acts is often as important as what he or she finds out. Professional conduct is an important value of journalism, and the way in which journalists conduct themselves has long-term implications for themselves and for the profession as a whole.

Information gathering, accuracy, verification and judging credibility – the major topics of the first sections in this book – are the professional goals of the journalists. Accomplishing these goals cannot be done by any means necessary, however.

They must be accompanied by a standard of conduct that brings credit to the journalist personally and enhances the credibility of the news organization for which the journalist works. The way in which journalists conduct themselves and the attitude and demeanor they bring to their jobs is as important as the information they gather.

None of this means that journalists must be universally popular or everlastingly lovable.

The product of their work, including the fact that they must sometimes tell uncomfortable truths, ensures that journalists will have opponents and even enemies. People will always want to keep information secret – information that should be made public – and they will not support efforts of journalists to reveal that information.

Sometimes, the public in general does not want information exposed because they perceive that it may reflects badly on society.

Given those pressures, journalists must not only act with the purest motives possible but must also observe the generally accepted rules of conduct for the profession.

The first tenet of that conduct is honesty. Journalists must be honest about who they are and what they are doing. In practical terms, this honesty means:

- Always revealing the fact that you are a journalist;
- Always telling sources what you are working on;
- Always informing sources that they might be quoted or that the information they give you might be used in an article.

In communicating with sources, reporters should say who they are at the beginning of the conversation, and they should explain what they are seeking and why. Journalists should seek consent from the sources in order to quote those sources or to use the information they give to the journalists. If the source does not give consent, the journalist should end the interview. (This does not mean that the journalist should stop seeking the information, however.)

In short, reporters should not use tricks or deception to get information.

Reports should not break the law. They should not steal. They should not trespass or break into an area where it is illegal for them to be.

Anonymous sources

A source will sometimes ask to remain anonymous or will promise information to the journalist only with the promise of anonymity. Journalists should not grant anonymity without careful consideration of the following points:

• Does the source really need to be anonymous?

• Using an anonymous source will likely hurt the credibility of the information and the credibility of the reporter.

• Is the news organization willing to support the reporter's promise of anonymity for the source?

• The legal implications of the granting of anonymity can be severe. Some reporters have gone to jail rather than go back on their words and reveal the source of the information to a prosecutor or judge. The reporter must ask, "Is this information worth going to jail for?"

Once a promise of anonymity is made, a reporter should not go back on his or her word.

We will discuss some of the legal aspects of confidentiality in a later section of this book.

Respect

One of the common images in television or movie depictions of reporters is that they are constantly sticking a microphone or a camera in the face of a bereaved or aggrieved person and asking, "How do you feel?"

In the real world, that rarely happens.

Reporters are human beings, too, and they are as reluctant as anyone else in approaching someone who has suffered a loss and talking with that person about the loss. Reporters understand that in such circumstances people are vulnerable and may be distrustful or easily upset.

Consequently, reporters learn to tread lightly, often showing great respect and deference to those in difficult situations. Those efforts can be rewarded. People suffering emotional pain or loss take some comfort in talking with a reporter about that loss because the reporter is trained to maintain a professional demeanor and can serve as an anchor for that person.

But journalists have to remember they have a job to do and that their ultimate duty is to their news organization and to their audience. Consequently, they cannot normally accede to requests by sources to withhold information that they have acquired legitimately and professionally.

Reporters must respect the people they come in contact with, but they must also respect the audience that depends on them for honest, accurate information. Reporters must obtain that information in a way that, if it came to light, would enhance their standing and credibility.

In class

Find a news story that uses anonymous sources. (Perhaps your instructor will provide you with one.) Why do you think the reporter agreed to leave the source's name out of the report? Do you think this was a good idea?

Ask yourself

List some of the circumstances where are journalist would not want to identify himself or herself as a journalist. Can you think of any?

1.7 Interviewing

Purpose of this section
To help students learn and practice the art and craft of interviewing.

Importance
Talking to people in order to get information from them is one of the basic techniques of a journalist. Learning to do this skillfully and efficiently is a basic part of the education of a journalist.

Do you know how to talk to people?

Of course, you say. I do it every day.

Yes, but do you REALLY know how to talk to people? Do you know how to listen? How to ask questions? How to follow up those questions with other questions?

Many professional journalists and journalism educators complain that high school and college students are bad interviewers because they simply do not know how to talk to people. Bob Steele, a member of the faculty at the Poynter Institute, wrote an article about interviewing in 2003 that drew a number of pointed comments about students who wanted to become journalists:

" . . . . *students often can't even, like, form a coherent sentence.*"

" . . . . *students are afraid of interviewing. I agree -- but not because they believe it to be an enterprise of rudeness.*"

"*. . . . I'm continually amazed that the lack of basic social and conversational skills among many, if not most, of my students.*"

"*Before I can teach interviewing, I have to teach them how to have civil conversations that actually use full sentences. I've even had to bring a telephone into a classroom and teach them how to use it in a professional manner.*"

"Their difficulties in conversational skills and inexperience in critical thinking makes teaching interviewing a frustrating experience."

"The art of interviewing is simply not taught in most journalism programs. It is not something you're born with. It is a craft that must be continually honed. The best professional experience I had was working for an executive producer who reviewed the interviews I field produced and gave me tips on everything from the length of my questions to the ethical nature of my approach."

Are you one of those students who can't form, like, a coherent sentence?

Conducting an interview with a source requires conducting background research beforehand to get a better handle on the subject matter. Conduct an interview with concise and poignant questions with tips from an award-winning journalist in this free video on journalism. **Watch this YouTube video from award-winning journalist Bruce Edwards.** *http://youtu.be/P_an_eC37eU*

Conducting an interview with a source requires conducting background research beforehand to get a better handle on the subject matter. Conduct an interview with concise and poignant questions with tips from an award-winning journalist in this free video on journalism. Watch this YouTube video from award-winning journalist Bruce Edwards.

Interviewing people is one of the most important things that a journalists do. Interviewing is the way they obtain most of their information for news stories. They don't watch television, and they don't look it up on the Internet. They talk to people.

Journalists have to overcome whatever shyness and insecurities they have about talking to people. They have to gain the confidence that people will help them out if those people are asked by someone who is intelligent, courteous and respectful.

Good interviewing begins with good conversation.

It should be generally enjoyable to all of those involved because information and ideas are exchanged. But the journalistic interview goes beyond good conversation because journalists are seeking information and asking questions that will elicit that information.

Good interviews are based on two things: the overall intelligence and demeanor of the reporter and the research that the reporter has done.

A journalists should know as much as possible about the person he or she is interviewing and about the topic of discussion. Sometimes students or beginning journalists believe they don't have to do much research because the person they are interviewing will tell them what they need to know or explain everything to them. Interviewees, then, are surprised and often irritated because they realize they are talking to someone who knows very little. The person being interviewed can feel like the journalist is lazy and simply wasting his or her time.

Sometimes, of course, with breaking news or deadline pressure, there isn't time to do much research before an interview has to be conducted. In those cases, journalists have to rely on their native intelligence and experience and on the demeanor they have developed to draw people into conversations.

As you learn and practice the art of interviewing, here are some things to remember:

• Prepare. Write out your questions. What information are you going to need to write a good story? Think about what your audience will want to know.

• Stay flexible. The interview may go in a different direction than what you planned. Be ready to respond to that.

• If you have to ask difficult questions, wait until the interview is nearly over.

• Note the surroundings and the characteristics of the interviewee.

• Develop a professional appearance and demeanor. Dress so that you represent yourself and your news organization well. Introduce yourself, shake hands if appropriate, and tell why you are there, even if the interviewee knows the reason.

• Learn how to ask questions – and then stop talking. Try to make your questions as short as possible, and don't be afraid to wait for an answer.

• Listen, listen, listen. Concentrate on what the interviewee has to say with everything you can muster. Listen for the substance of what he or she is saying, but also remember that you need words and sentences you can put into direct quotations.

• Housekeeping duties. Ask your interviewee how to spell his or her name (always), and also ask for the person's exact title. Ask for permission to call back if there is information that you need.

• The key to a good interview is being interested in what the interviewee has to say and being confident that the interviewee will talk to you.

Interviewing is a skill that can be developed and practiced immediately. Don't wait until you feel more prepared. Start right now.

In class

Select the oldest and wisest member of your family. Conduct a formal interview with that person about what he or she remembers as a child. To make it formal, schedule a time for the interview and make a list of questions that your instructor can review before the interview is conducted. Record the interview if possible.

Ask yourself

OK, so, like, are you one of those people the text talks about when it says this:

Are you one of those students who can't form, like, a coherent sentence?

Assess your ability to speak clearly, coherently and efficiently. What are your strengths? What are your weaknesses? Where can you improve?

Record yourself speaking formally – maybe reciting the Gettysburg Address -- for about two minutes. Make a list of the characteristics of your voice and the way you speak. This may be somewhat painful, but you should try to listen to yourself as closely as possible.

1.8 Public information

Purpose of this section
To give students a sense of what stored source information is available to them to use as journalists.

Importance
Stored source information constitutes a vast and valuable pool of information that journalists use in their work every day. But this information needs to be treated carefully and professionally.

Never has so much information been so readily and quickly available to many people. Never.

Barely two decades ago, to have such a vast amount of material accessible through a computer and keyboard on one's desk was almost inconceivable. And that pool of information is growing by the minute.

Does having this much stored information make the journalist's job of reporting harder or easier? Both.

Journalists have more information than ever to work with, but they also have more information to assess and decipher. As with anyone else who has a high-speed Internet connection, a good search engine, and a few key terms, journalists can be quickly overwhelmed with information – or, at least, the possibilities of information.

Journalists conquer this mountain of data with a few principles, some basic understanding of stored information and some procedural standards:

Not all information that is stored and available is equal. Some of it is good and useful. Some of it – sometimes a great deal of it – is not. Here are some of the problems that journalists find with stored information:

- Some of it is simply wrong.

- Stored information sources may be incomplete or misfiled or mis-categorized.
- Some information may be out of date.
- Some stored information may be easy to misinterpret because it lacks the proper context.

Permission to use information generally available to the public is usually not required. That is to say that if you can find it as a journalist, you can use the information. You do not have to ask permission to do so. But, as a journalist you must attribute information to its source – that is, you have to tell where you got the information – and if you are going to quote the information directly (use the exact words of the source) you have to use quotation marks around those words and tell where they came from. Journalists (and students) who do not follow this procedure can be guilty of plagiarism.

This does not apply to pictures. If you want to use a picture, you should always – always – ask permission from the person or organization that owns the picture.

Information from expert or official sources is preferred. We discussed what we mean by "expert" and "official" in a previous section. Many of the references there applied to people. The same things can be said about stored information. For instance, information that has passed muster from government, university or scholarly web sites and other sources is sought out by journalists over information presented by those who have no or few credentials.

The more recent the information, the better – usually. Journalists want the most up-to-date information that is available. Timeliness is important to the journalist. It may also be assumed that the latest information will include or take into account earlier information. But as with all information, journalists need to be careful in their research and check earlier versions of information if they are available to see if there are changes, contradictions or corrections.

Information gleaned from various sources is generally better than information from a single source. As with information from people, information from stored sources has more credibility if it comes from various sources or is confirmed by independent sources. To read the same thing in two different books by two authors who have no connection with each other enhances the information's reliability. Journalists should actively try to confirm information if that is possible.

Good journalists who gather information from stored sources usually try to confirm it with a personal source. Having a person verify the information that you are reading helps its believability. Plus, the person can clarify and expand the information and possibly can provide even more up-to-date information.

Information from stored sources need to be attributed, just as information from live sources needs attribution. Part of the journalist's job, as we have said over and over, is to verify information and to tell the audience where that information comes from. That is the discipline of journalism that separates it from other forms of communication. This applies as much to stored information as it does to information from any other source.

Skepticism. Just as journalists have it for what they hear from sources, they should also have it for what they read from stored sources. Just because something is written down in a book or magazine or posted on a web site does not mean that it is correct. Journalists should always be looking for the flaws, shortcoming, or lack of logic in anything they read.

Journalists and the general public have the right to some information. Some of this information comes from government sources, and it is the responsibility of government organizations to make it available. The Federal government has the Freedom of Information Act that mandates that government agencies respond to requests for information. Journalists have used the Freedom of Information Act to get a wide variety of records and documents that agencies have created or collected.

Many state and local governments have similar laws that tell city and county agencies, school boards, zoning boards and other governmental groups that they must provide information to the public about what they are doing and what policies they are making. These laws are generally grouped under the name of open records laws, and journalists should be familiar with the laws in their states and local areas.

In general, the legal system in America is an open one. That is, you can attend a trial or court hearing and you can see certain court documents without asking for any special permission. It is important for the legal system to operate in the open so that people will believe that it is fair and that the laws are being applied impartially. While there are some instances where court hearings are closed – most notably when juveniles are charged with a crime – courts and court records remain available to the public.

Watch the video of Dr. David Cullier speaking about access to public information, which can be found at https://vimeo.com/15412063.

Finally, laws demand that many businesses provide information to the public. For instance, any company that has publicly traded stock must publish an annual report, and that report must contain certain information about the company's operation, including general financial information. Organizations that have non-profit status are also required to disclose certain information about how they operate, who is in charge, and how much money those people make. Again, journalists should be familiar with the laws concerning these requirements as they seek information in their reporting.

In class

Not everything – not yet, at least – is available on the Internet. Can you think of any information a journalist would want that is not available on the web?

Ask yourself

Try to find all of the publicly available information about yourself and your immediate family. How would you go about it? Discuss this with your teacher and classmates to see what ideas they have. Then try to find what you can.

Sidebar:

John F. Kennedy on the importance of open government

In April 1961, a few months after taking office as president of the United States, John F. Kennedy spoke to the American Newspaper Publishers Association about the importance of maintaining an open government.

In the speech he said, "The very word 'secrecy' is repugnant in a free and open society; and we are as a people inherently and historically opposed to secret societies, to secret oaths and to secret proceedings."

Entire Text Transcript Of Speech

Mr. Chairman, ladies and gentlemen:

I appreciate very much your generous invitation to be here tonight.

You bear heavy responsibilities these days and an article I read some time ago reminded me of how particularly heavily the burdens of present day events bear upon your profession.

You may remember that in 1851 the New York Herald Tribune under the sponsorship and publishing of Horace Greeley, employed as its London correspondent an obscure journalist by the name of Karl Marx.

We are told that foreign correspondent Marx, stone broke, and with a family ill and undernourished, constantly appealed to Greeley and managing editor Charles Dana for an increase in his munificent salary of $5 per installment, a salary which he and Engels ungratefully labeled as the "lousiest petty bourgeois cheating."

But when all his financial appeals were refused, Marx looked around for other means of livelihood and fame, eventually terminating his relationship with the Tribune and devoting his talents full time to the cause that would bequeath the world the seeds of Leninism, Stalinism, revolution and the cold war.

If only this capitalistic New York newspaper had treated him more kindly; if only Marx had remained a foreign correspondent, history might have been different. And I hope all publishers will bear this lesson in mind the next time they receive a poverty-stricken appeal for a small increase in the expense account from an obscure newspaper man.

I have selected as the title of my remarks tonight "The President and the Press." Some may suggest that this would be more naturally worded "The President Versus the Press." But those are not my sentiments tonight.

It is true, however, that when a well-known diplomat from another country demanded recently that our State Department repudiate certain newspaper attacks on his colleague it was unnecessary for us to reply that this Administration was not responsible for the press, for the press had already made it clear that it was not responsible for this Administration.

Nevertheless, my purpose here tonight is not to deliver the usual assault on the so-called one party press. On the contrary, in recent months I have rarely heard any complaints about political bias in the press except from a few Republicans. Nor is it my purpose tonight to discuss or defend the televising of Presidential press conferences. I think it is highly beneficial to have some 20,000,000 Americans regularly sit in on these conferences to observe, if I may say so, the incisive, the intelligent and the courteous qualities displayed by your Washington correspondents.

Nor, finally, are these remarks intended to examine the proper degree of privacy which the press should allow to any President and his family.

If in the last few months your White House reporters and photographers have been attending church services with regularity, that has surely done them no harm.

On the other hand, I realize that your staff and wire service photographers may be complaining that they do not enjoy the same green privileges at the local golf courses that they once did.

It is true that my predecessor did not object as I do to pictures of one's golfing skill in action. But neither on the other hand did he ever bean a Secret Service man.

My topic tonight is a more sober one of concern to publishers as well as editors.

I want to talk about our common responsibilities in the face of a common danger. The events of recent weeks may have helped to illuminate that challenge for some; but the dimensions of its threat have loomed large on the horizon for many years. Whatever our hopes may be for the future--for reducing this threat or living with it--there is no escaping either the gravity or the totality of its challenge to our survival and to our security--a challenge that confronts us in unaccustomed ways in every sphere of human activity.

This deadly challenge imposes upon our society two requirements of direct concern both to the press and to the President--two requirements that may seem almost contradictory in tone, but which must be reconciled and fulfilled if we are to meet this national peril. I refer, first, to the need for a far greater public information; and, second, to the need for far greater official secrecy.

The very word "secrecy" is repugnant in a free and open society; and we are as a people inherently and historically opposed to secret societies, to secret oaths and to secret proceedings. We decided long ago that the dangers of excessive and unwarranted concealment of pertinent facts far outweighed the dangers which are cited to justify it. Even today, there is little value in opposing the threat of a closed society by imitating its arbitrary restrictions. Even today, there is little value in insuring the survival of our nation if our traditions do not survive with it. And there is very grave danger that an announced need for increased security will be seized upon by those anxious to expand its meaning to the very limits of official censorship and concealment. That I do not intend to permit to the extent that it is in my control. And no official of my Administration, whether his rank is high or low, civilian or military, should interpret my words here tonight as an excuse to censor the news, to stifle dissent, to cover up our mistakes or to withhold from the press and the public the facts they deserve to know.

But I do ask every publisher, every editor, and every newsman in the nation to reexamine his own standards, and to recognize the nature of our country's peril. In time of war, the government and the press have customarily joined in an effort based largely on self-discipline, to prevent unauthorized disclosures to the enemy. In time of "clear and present danger," the courts have held that even the privileged rights of the First Amendment must yield to the public's need for national security.

Today no war has been declared--and however fierce the struggle may be, it may never be declared in the traditional fashion. Our way of life is under attack. Those who make themselves our enemy are advancing around the globe. The survival of our friends is in danger. And yet no war has been declared, no borders have been crossed by marching troops, no missiles have been fired.

If the press is awaiting a declaration of war before it imposes the self-discipline of combat conditions, then I can only say that no war ever posed a greater threat to our security. If you are awaiting a finding of "clear and present danger," then I can only say that the danger has never been more clear and its presence has never been more imminent.

It requires a change in outlook, a change in tactics, a change in missions--by the government, by the people, by every businessman or labor leader, and by every newspaper. For we are opposed around the world by a monolithic and ruthless conspiracy that relies primarily on covert means for expanding its sphere of influence--on infiltration instead of invasion, on subversion instead of elections, on intimidation instead of free choice, on guerrillas by night instead of armies by day. It is a system which has conscripted vast human and material resources into the building of a tightly knit, highly efficient machine that combines military, diplomatic, intelligence, economic, scientific and political operations.

Its preparations are concealed, not published. Its mistakes are buried, not headlined. Its dissenters are silenced, not praised. No expenditure is questioned, no rumor is printed, no secret is revealed. It conducts the Cold War, in short, with a war-time discipline no democracy would ever hope or wish to match.

Nevertheless, every democracy recognizes the necessary restraints of national security--and the question remains whether those restraints need to be more strictly observed if we are to oppose this kind of attack as well as outright invasion.

For the facts of the matter are that this nation's foes have openly boasted of acquiring through our newspapers information they would otherwise hire agents to acquire through theft, bribery or espionage; that details of this nation's covert preparations to counter the enemy's covert operations have been available to every newspaper reader, friend and foe alike; that the size, the strength, the location and the nature of our forces and weapons, and our plans and strategy for their use, have all been pinpointed in the press and other news media to a degree sufficient to satisfy any foreign power; and that, in at least in one case, the publication of details concerning a secret mechanism whereby satellites were followed required its alteration at the expense of considerable time and money.

The newspapers which printed these stories were loyal, patriotic, responsible and well-meaning. Had we been engaged in open warfare, they undoubtedly would not have published such items. But in the absence of open warfare, they recognized only the tests of journalism and not the tests of national security. And my question tonight is whether additional tests should not now be adopted.

The question is for you alone to answer. No public official should answer it for you. No governmental plan should impose its restraints against your will. But I would be failing in my duty to the nation, in considering all of the responsibilities that we now bear and all of the means at hand to meet those responsibilities, if I did not commend this problem to your attention, and urge its thoughtful consideration.

On many earlier occasions, I have said--and your newspapers have constantly said--that these are times that appeal to every citizen's sense of sacrifice and self-discipline. They call out to every citizen to weigh his rights and comforts against his obligations to the common good. I cannot now believe that those citizens who serve in the newspaper business consider themselves exempt from that appeal.

I have no intention of establishing a new Office of War Information to govern the flow of news. I am not suggesting any new forms of censorship or any new types of security classifications. I have no easy answer to the dilemma that I have posed, and would not seek to impose it if I had one. But I am asking the members of the newspaper profession and the industry in this country to reexamine their own responsibilities, to consider the degree and the nature of the present danger, and to heed the duty of self-restraint which that danger imposes upon us all.

Every newspaper now asks itself, with respect to every story: "Is it news?" All I suggest is that you add the question: "Is it in the interest of the national security?" And I hope that every group in America--unions and businessmen and public officials at every level-- will ask the same question of their endeavors, and subject their actions to the same exacting tests.

And should the press of America consider and recommend the voluntary assumption of specific new steps or machinery, I can assure you that we will cooperate whole-heartedly with those recommendations.

Perhaps there will be no recommendations. Perhaps there is no answer to the dilemma faced by a free and open society in a cold and secret war. In times of peace, any discussion of this subject, and any action that results, are both painful and without precedent. But this is a time of peace and peril which knows no precedent in history.

It is the unprecedented nature of this challenge that also gives rise to your second obligation--an obligation which I share. And that is our obligation to inform and alert the American people--to make certain that they possess all the facts that they need, and understand them as well--the perils, the prospects, the purposes of our program and the choices that we face.

No President should fear public scrutiny of his program. For from that scrutiny comes understanding; and from that understanding comes support or opposition. And both are necessary. I am not asking your newspapers to support the Administration, but I am asking your help in the tremendous task of informing and alerting the American people. For I have complete confidence in the response and dedication of our citizens whenever they are fully informed.

I not only could not stifle controversy among your readers--I welcome it. This Administration intends to be candid about its errors; for as a wise man once said: "An error does not become a mistake until you refuse to correct it." We intend to accept full responsibility for our errors; and we expect you to point them out when we miss them.

Without debate, without criticism, no Administration and no country can succeed--and no republic can survive. That is why the Athenian lawmaker Solon decreed it a crime for any citizen to shrink from controversy. And that is why our press was protected by the First Amendment-- the only business in America specifically protected by the Constitution- -not primarily to amuse and entertain, not to emphasize the trivial and the sentimental, not to simply "give the public what it wants"--but to inform, to arouse, to reflect, to state our dangers and our opportunities, to indicate our crises and our choices, to lead, mold, educate and sometimes even anger public opinion.

This means greater coverage and analysis of international news--for it is no longer far away and foreign but close at hand and local. It means greater attention to improved understanding of the news as well as improved transmission. And it means, finally, that government at all levels, must meet its obligation to provide you with the fullest possible information outside the narrowest limits of national security--and we intend to do it.

It was early in the Seventeenth Century that Francis Bacon remarked on three recent inventions already transforming the world: the compass, gunpowder and the printing press. Now the links between the nations first forged by the compass have made us all citizens of the world, the hopes and threats of one becoming the hopes and threats of us all. In that one world's efforts to live together, the evolution of gunpowder to its ultimate limit has warned mankind of the terrible consequences of failure.

And so it is to the printing press--to the recorder of man's deeds, the keeper of his conscience, the courier of his news--that we look for strength and assistance, confident that with your help man will be what he was born to be: free and independent.

http://www.jfklibrary.org/Researchold/Ready-Reference/JFK-Speeches/The-President-and-the-Press-Address-before-the-American-Newspaper-Publishers-Association.aspx

1.9 Observation

Purpose of this section
To show students that covering live events is part of a reporter's daily life and to offer some ways that journalists prepare to do that.

Importance
News reporters are the eyes and ears of their audience at many of the events that are important and of interest to news consumers. Covering an event takes special commitment and energy on the part of the journalist.

Reporters are trained to be observers, to witness those events that the general public cannot attend. Ultimately, reporters prove their worth and the value of the profession of journalism by being where news is happening and by interpreting those events for the audience.

Television cameras operated by videographers and video cameras operated by amateurs are ubiquitous. Rarely does anything of any importance, it seems, occur without be captured on camera.

But pictures, even moving pictures, can only tell us so much about an event and can add just a limited amount to our understanding of the things that happen in our world. We need reporters to identify, to explain, to offer background, and to give us context for what we may see.

Being there is part of the reporter's job.

But on-the-scene reporting is not an easy task. It demands training, experience, planning, intellectual acumen and physical energy. To cover an event well, reporters must plan as much as possible, they must use their instincts to find out the information they need, and they have to rely on the experience they have acquired as journalists. All of these things make great demands on reporters.

Three kinds of events occur that reporters must cover: staged events; spontaneous events; and events that are a mixture of the two.

A **staged event** is one that is planned and about which information can be gained before the event occurs. A staged event might be a concert, a political speech, an awards ceremony or a grand opening. These events are usually managed by a person or organization and have a purpose that benefits whoever is producing the event. These are the easiest for the journalist to plan, often because the producers of the event want news coverage and will be cooperative with the journalists.

Journalists who cover staged events should contact the producers beforehand to get the who, what, when and where of the event. They should make sure that there are arrangements to accommodate journalists by finding out what access journalists will have to the areas of the event, to whom the journalists can talk to, the timing and scheduling of the event and so on.

Journalists should check with the producers to see if there are any special rules in covering the event and to see if those rules are acceptable. Sometimes producers will want to limit coverage or will try to make sure that events are reported in a particular way. Journalists should not agree to attend and cover staged events if the conditions intrude on their freedom to write and say what they want about the event.

One particularly important thing to check on with a staged event is to find what electronic and wireless availability there is in case journalists want to report live from the scene via the web.

A **spontaneous event** is when something unexpected and significant occurs that involves more than a few people: a fire, an explosion at a factory, a major traffic jam caused by a wreck, a tornado that destroys property, etc. While many spontaneous events are bad news, that is not always the case.

Still, a spontaneous event is more likely to involve tragedy than not. Journalists must be ready to cover such events with all of the professionalism and objectivity they can display. They must remember that they are witnesses and should not get caught up in the moment and its emotions.

In covering a spontaneous event, journalists should try to get as close to the event's location as possible. When the event is a crime or natural disaster, this may not be easy, and journalists should always carry some form of identification that shows they are reporters working as media professionals. Police and emergency workers are more cooperative in allowing reporters access when they are convinced the reporters are professionals.

On September 11, 2001, CNN reporter David Mattingly was visiting family in Pennsylvania when he hear the news of the terrorist attacks in New York and Washington. He then realized he was about two hours away from where a plane hijacked by terrorists had crashed. He drove there immediately but did not have any identification that would show he was a reporter. He talked with the police guarding the crash scene and convinced them to let him have access to the scene by showing them his Georgia license tags (CNN headquarters is in Atlanta) and a CNN baseball cap that he had in the back seat of his vehicle. (See James Glen Stovall, *Journalism: Who, What, When, Where, Why and How*, Allyn and Bacon, 2005.)

Reporters covering spontaneous events try to find officials in charge of the scene so they can get the latest information. They also try to find eyewitnesses to the event and interview them. Finally, they try to find people who have been affected by the event and talk with them about the ways in which the event has altered their lives.

As with any interview situation, journalists should identify themselves and make sure that people understand they are talking with a member of the news media and that they may be quoted if they continue the conversation. Journalists should take additional care for those who are grieving and not take advantage of their vulnerability. And, if journalists are asked by those in grief to be left alone, they should honor that request.

A **mixed event** is one that has both elements of spontaneity and planning. An event might be planned, but its outcome may be in doubt. A sporting event such as football game is a good example. Journalists know generally what will happen at such events, but they still need to be there to witness the action and record the outcome.

In class

Watch a live sports event on television and pretend that you are reporting on that event for a web site that is being constantly updated. As the event is occurring, try to write down the things that happened. Do this for an inning of a baseball game or a series of downs for a football game. Did you find it difficult? Why was it hard?

Ask yourself

A. Do you enjoy going places, meeting people, seeing things as they happen. If so, you probably would be a good on-the-scene reporter. Not everyone is like that. Whom do you know who would enjoy doing this? What kind of personality do you have to have to do this?

B. Have you or anyone in your family witnessed a non-sporting news event – a flood or a fire or a robbery or something of that nature? What was it like?

1.10 Linking

Purpose of this section

To emphasize to students the importance of finding good links for their stories in order to direct readers to other relevant, useful and interesting information.

Importance

Linking has become one of the most important skills that a reporter can acquire. Finding good, relevant links enriches the articles that the reporter researches and enhances the experience of the reader. It has become an integral task of the journalist in this age of web journalism.

Linking is the simplest, most basic tool of hypertext.

By using it properly, journalists can offer readers far more than what they can gather and process through their efforts. Reporters can enhance the reader's experience and can perform a valuable service for the reader by pointing the reader to relevant sources of additional information.

Journalists can do all of this. Unfortunately, far too often, they do not.

Why journalists fail to harness the power of linking in their news reports may come from a variety of reasons and practices. Journalists are often trained to think of their work as autonomous – not connected with other information or sources except as they are included in the narrative the journalist writes. Finding and assessing good links takes time, something a reporting working under deadline pressure may not have. News organizations do not encourage linking in their general practices and, in fact, may actively discourage it. In addition, reporters and editors may not know enough about HTML to use it to build links for their stories. Finally, many journalists simply do not understand the power of linking and what it can do for the reader.

All of these reasons and practices could be corrected easily – and they should be. Linking is too valuable for the reader and too important for the journalist to be ignored. As well as offering a valuable service to the reader, links tap into the interactivity function of the web, allowing the users to have some control over what they see and how they navigate through the information that the journalist is providing.

Putting a link into a story or listing links at the end of a story calls for only the very minimum of knowledge about HTML (hypertext mark-up language). The tag for linking is <a href=> followed by the web address of the information or page you want to link to. This should be placed before the word or words that will appear as the link on the web page. Immediately after those words should be an end tag, in this case </a>. That's it. That is all the technical expertise that is required.

But while creating links is a relatively simple matter, the art of linking takes a delicate and skillful hand and a resourceful and agile brain. Links should be carefully assessed for what they will mean to a reader and how they will add to the overall package of information the journalist is providing for the reader.

Links do not serve this purpose if they are any of the following:

• **Opaque or unexplained.** It should be obvious to a reasonably intelligent reader what he or she will be getting when a link is clicked. Sometimes this is evident from the content surrounding the link or from the name of the link itself. Too often, however, it is not obvious, and the reader is left to guess.

• **Too general.** A link that simply takes someone to the home page of a web site when the relevant information is somewhere within the web site makes the reader work too hard. The reporter and editor should do the heavy lifting in terms of locating information and pointing the reader specifically to that information.

• **Irrelevant.** Some links may be full of information, but they are not germane to the point of story. In these cases, they should not be included.

• **Commercial.** Links should not take readers to sites that are advertisements or that ask them to spend their money unless paid links are clearly marked. Currently, many book titles that are made into links take the reader to the book's page on Amazon or some other commercial site. These undescribed links do not give the reader much information but instead waste the reader's time.

• **Dead or rotting.** One of the judgments a reporter or editor must make about links is how long they are likely to remain live. Many newspaper web sites put their stories behind a firewall after a certain amount of time, and a link to that site will give the reader nothing unless he or she is registered with the site or subscribes to the site. "Link rot," as it is called, should be a major concern to editors, and they should think about the long-term value of their stories.

Outside the links on the navigation bar, two types of links are most common in news reporting: inline links and link lists.

An inline link takes the words of a story and makes them into a link. The link is recognizable by a different coloring of the type (commonly blue, but not always) and offers the reader of the story a way to get additional information instantly. Inline linking is an efficient way of providing links for the reader, but there are some considerations that reporters and editors much make if they are to be used:

- Only a few words should be used as a link (three to five at the most); otherwise, the link is distracting.
- It should be obvious from the context or the words themselves where the link is going and what the reader will find there.
- Inline links invite the reader to interrupt reading the narrative the reporter has written. Do the reporter and editor really want this to happen?
- Unless there is a compelling reason to do otherwise, no paragraph should have more than one or two inline links.

A link list can be placed at any appropriate place on the page – even inside a story as long as it does not confuse the reader. The link list is not as efficient as inline linking, but it has the potential of offering the reader more information about the links. Also, unlike inline linking, it does not require the writer to compose the narrative in such a way as to explain the links.

Both inline linking and link lists have their advantages, and news organizations should consider using both, even on the same page.

Linking is so basic to the web that it should be a natural and integral part of the reporting and editing process of web journalism.

In class

Select a news story from a major news organization (*New York Times, Fox News, Washington Post,* etc.) and find links that, if the organizations included them in the story or in a list beside the story, would be use for the reader. Include with each link the following:

-- the name of the site being linked to

-- a short description of what the reader will find there

-- the URL or web address <http://www . . .>

Ask yourself

What topic interests you the most? Where would you go to find information about that topic if you knew little or nothing about it? Who are the people and organizations that would know the most about that topic?

1.11 Confidentiality

Purpose of this section
To introduce to students some of the important legal concepts surrounding newsgathering, particularly the idea of confidentiality and reporter's privilege.

Importance
Students must understand that while the First Amendment grants the right of free speech and free press, journalists must always be aware that some laws, traditions and precedents will govern their actions.

Most of the time, when reporters talk to people and ask them for information, those conversations are "on the record." That is, what the source tells the reporter can be reported, and the reporter can use the name of the source to attribute the information.

Sometimes, however, things are not so open.

Let's say, for instance, that a person works for a company that is doing something illegal. That person wants to expose the legality but does not want to lose her job. She might go to a reporter with the information and ask that the reporter keep her name out of the news article.

The reporter agrees and promises the source confidentiality. They have made a confidentiality agreement. The reporter publishes the article about the illegality but does not name the source of the information. A prosecutor reads the article and decides to prosecute the people who are committing the illegal acts. The prosecutors asks the reporter for the name of the person who is the source of the information.

The reporter refuses, citing the confidentiality agreement.

A judge agrees with the prosecutor and orders the reporter to reveal the source of the information, saying that if the reporter does not, the reporter will go to jail for contempt of court.

What should the reporter do – break his word to the source and violate the confidentiality agreement or keep his word, refuse to reveal the source and risk going to jail?

When communication between people is outside the reach of the legal system, it is called privilege. Laws in the United States recognize some relationships as having an absolute privilege (they cannot be violated under any circumstances) or limited privilege (only certain types of information are privileged.) Some of those relationships include:

- **Husband-wife.** No court can compel spouses to reveal what they say to each other.
- **Priest-confessor.** People who are recognized as priests, clerics or ministers cannot reveal what people tell them in a religious, counseling or confessional setting.
- **Doctor-patient.** What you tell your doctor, and what he or she may tell you remains between the two of you. Medical information in general is considered to be among the most privileged information there is.
- **Lawyer-client.** A criminal can confess a crime to a lawyer, but the lawyer cannot tell anyone about that confession. Almost all communication between an attorney and a client is privileged.

Many journalists believe that conversations between reporters and sources should be privileged. In fact, they go further by asserting that the newsgathering process should be free of intrusion by government officials. This means that notes and other materials that reporters have gathered, as well as their sources, should be beyond the reach of the legal system unless the journalists themselves choose to reveal them.

Journalists argue that some privilege is necessary for them to do their jobs effectively and that the First Amendment – with its assurance of freedom of the press – is the legal basis for this assertion. They believe that the intent of the writers of the Constitution was to protect the press from intrusion by the government. Allowing journalists to offer confidentiality agreements in situations such as the one described at the beginning of this section is one way of expanding the powers of the First Amendment. Journalists should be able to gather information without the fear of going to jail if they refuse to reveal their sources.

Most journalists who make this argument want a limited privilege, not an absolute privilege.

Arguments against giving journalists this kind of privilege come most often from lawyers and prosecutors. They say that sometimes reporters have information that is necessary for prosecuting criminals or for assuring that the courts can guarantee a fair trial. A journalist might hold a key piece of information that could put away a dangerous criminal or exonerate a person accused of a crime.

Over many years of debate about this topic, more than 30 states have agreed with journalists' arguments and have granted to journalists a limited privilege. Under certain circumstances, they can refuse to reveal the names of sources or certain other information if they feel their ability to gather news would be compromised. These laws – which are call shield laws – give journalists some protection if they are involved with cases in local or state courts.

The federal government, however, does not have a shield law for journalists. Consequently, in cases that go before federal courts, journalists do not have any legal privilege. In a number of cases, journalists have spent time in jail for contempt of court because they would not reveal the source of their information.

Even though they have the law to back them up, prosecutors often shy away from demanding that journalists reveal their sources. Such demands draw a lot of publicity and may distract them from some of the more central parts of their cases. And, if the journalist refuses to reveal the information, bringing them before a judge and convincing the judge that such information is necessary is a long and difficult process.

Interestingly, some journalists to do not believe that the state or government should offer a shield law to journalists. They argue the following points:

• Governments should not be involved in "protecting" the newsgathering process. Sometimes governmental protection means that the government can have control of it.

• Shield laws necessarily define who the journalist is; they say who has the privilege and who doesn't. Journalists do not like the fact that the government says who can and can't be a journalist.

• The First Amendment offers the protection of free speech and free press to every citizen, not just the people who gather news as a profession or the organizations that deem themselves as the news media.

The arguments about confidentiality and reporter's privilege go on all the time, and they will probably never be completely resolved.

How do you feel about them?

In class

Find a journalist whom you can interview about this topic. Ask him or her about confidential sources:

• Have you ever used confidential sources?

• How do you feel about using them?

• What are the drawbacks to using them?

Assess what you find out with the information in this module. Do you think using confidential sources is a good practice for journalists?

Ask yourself

A. Considering the arguments presented in this section, do you think that a shield law for journalists is a good thing or not a good thing?

B. Does your state have a shield law? If not, what is the state that is closest to yours that does have a shield law?

C. Can you imagine a situation where you, as a student journalist, would want to offer a confidentiality agreement to a source? Remember that such an agreement is very serious and should only be offered after you have given it a good deal of thought.

D. List some of the reasons why journalists should feel so strongly about not breaking confidentiality agreements.

1.12 Ethics: Covering tragedy

Purpose of this section
To orient students to the fact that tragedy is a part of journalism and reporters must deal with tragic events and those caught up in them in an ethical, humane and professional manner.

Importance
Every reporter has to deal with tragedy and with the people who are involved in tragic events. Accidents and loss are part of the fabric of society, and those stories must be told.

Tragedy and loss are part of the lives of individuals and of society as a whole. No matter how hard we try, we cannot escape them. Bad things happen. Bad people do bad things. No amount of planning and precaution can shield us from them.

Tragedy and loss are part of the professional life of the journalist. For media consumers, tragedy makes a compelling story when those stories can be viewed from afar. Unfortunately, journalists cannot view them from afar. They must get close enough to see, hear and smell the remains of tragedy. They must talk to the people who have experienced the loss and to the people who are helping those people deal with it. They must view the effects of tragic and heart-breaking events and then describe those events for a larger audience.

Tragedy often is sudden and unexpected. No one foresees it clearly, and therefore planning for it is always inadequate. Tragic events are likely to impose massive losses on people and emotional costs that most find incomprehensible and overwhelming.

Consequently, it is important for journalists to take the following into consideration when they have to cover tragic events:

A journalist's first obligation and major responsibility is to gather accurate and complete information so that the full story can be told. The truth honors people who are experiencing a tragedy. Journalists not only have a responsibility to their audience to present accurate information, but they also have a responsibility to those involved to do so.

Journalists should maintain a sense of distance and professionalism about their work and their situation. Reporters are human beings, certainly, but when tragedy occurs, they should not allow empathy to cloud their thinking or their actions. If they can relieve immediate suffering by lending a hand, they should certainly do so. But they are not professional rescue or aid workers. They are there to do a job that has broader implications.

Journalists should do their jobs as unobtrusively as possible. They should be keenly aware of what police, rescue and aid workers are doing and should try to observe from a close distance. They should not get in the way.

Treating everyone involved with a tragedy – victims, aid workers, bystanders – with respect and consideration should be an ongoing practice of journalists. The reporter has an important job to do, but he or she is not the most important person at the scene.

Journalists have a right to be where tragedies have occurred. They should respect lines of authority and the limits of being on private property, but they should not be intimidated and told that they are not welcome. Police and firefighters sometimes overstep their authority by telling journalists that they have no right to take pictures or interview victims. That is simply not the case, and officials have no enforceable authority in this regard.

Letting people talk and tell their stories is one of the most useful things a journalist can do. Sometimes, people caught up in tragic events do not want to talk, and journalists should respect that and not badger them. Often, however, contrary to what you might have seen in movie depictions, victims do want to tell their stories and are genuinely appreciative of journalists who ask questions and are interested in what they have to say.

Journalists should follow up with the victims of tragedies in the days and weeks after the event has occurred. The full impact of a loss may be felt only after some time has passed, and victims appreciate a call or visit to see how they are coping and what effect the event has had on their lives. At this point, journalists can help them give voice to their loss and their feelings about it.

Covering tragic events is never easy. But journalists can ease the burdens of the victims and can render a service to society by doing it well and by acting professionally.

In class

A. Read the news reports of a tragic event that has occurred in your area. (See the list at the beginning of the text for anything like that which might have occurred near you.) Note the information that the reporters has gathered, and from the report itself, try to get an idea of the people the reporter talked with.

B. After completing part A of these section, try to get in touch with the reporter and talk with him or her about what it was like to cover this story. Ask what it was like at the scene and the people the reporter talked with to get the information. Who are the people who would talk to the reporter and who would not? How did they react to having a reporter on the scene?

Ask yourself

A. Many journalists find that covering disaster, death and tragedy is something they are not cut out for. How about you? Are you the kind of person who could enter a disaster scene and maintain professionalism and objectivity?

In the middle of a tragedy

Dr. Mark Harmon, a journalism professor at the University of Tennessee describes what it was like to be involved in a tragic news event, not as a journalist but as a participant. Watch the video here:

https://vimeo.com/5836010

2. Deadline reporting

One of the things that distinguishes journalism is that information must be processed and delivered to an audience quickly. Journalists do not have the luxury of time. The emergence of the web as a news medium has put greater emphasis on this aspect of the profession.

2.1 Types of stories

Purpose of this section
To introduce to students some of concepts and practices of deadline reporting.

Importance
Deadline reporting – covering an event immediately or as it happens – is one of the aspects of journalism that makes it different from other forms of communication.

Covering news on a daily -- or hourly -- basis is one of the great and common challenges that a reporter faces. The ability to respond quickly to events, even as they are occurring, to gather information and to put that information into a form appropriate for a news medium is a much-valued talent in journalism. Websites and Twitter offer all news organizations the ability to generate news immediately, and news consumers want their news the moment it happens.

The following are some of the kinds of stories that can be produced on a daily basis:

Evergreen. These are stories that can be worked on at any time and published and distributed at any time. They are feature stories that are not likely to go out of date in the near future. They are what the daily reporter works on when the types of stories listed below are not in play.

Currency stories. These are stories about current issues or controversies that are not necessarily tied to a physical event. The major news value here is currency (thus the name) – what people are doing, talking about and thinking about at the moment. They include localizing state, national and international stories as well as stories about local issues. They may be "seasonal," such as the beginning of the semester, spring break or final exam week.

Planned events. Speeches, meetings, announcements and other such events come under this heading. These are legitimate stories to cover that give us a sense of the normal life of the campus. Just because they are planned, however, does not always make them predictable. For instance, we may know that someone is going to

66

give a speech, but we do not know what that person will say. Still, planned events can provide some predictability for our breaking news week.

Unplanned events. These events constitute the heart of breaking news and are of the highest value to the news organization. They are the opportunity for a news organization to demonstrate its worth to its audience. Covering significant, unplanned events should be the major focus of our efforts to teach students about breaking news. These events include fires, power outages, accidents, traffic disruptions, crimes, police alerts, University announcements (particularly from the chancellor or president) and the like.

2.2 Covering breaking news

Students should learn to do three things with regard to breaking news: recognize, assess and respond.

Recognize. Journalists should sensitize themselves to the possibility that they may be in the middle or a breaking news story. Or what they hear about from someone else may be a breaking news story. They may be walking down the street and hear an ambulance or firetruck. They may be sitting in a class and a professor says something about what has just happened or what he or she has just seen or heard.

This sensitivity should be based on an understanding of traditional news values: currency, prominence, timeliness, impact, conflict, proximity and unusualness. Because journalists are reporting locally, they should recognize that news they should be investigating and reporting on may be -- and probably is -- within arm's length.

Assess. The student journalist (those likely to be reading this book) should assess the initial information he or she acquires that might become a breaking news story. First, is the information initially credible? Does it sound as if it might be correct?

Second, does it contain one of the news values listed above? Timeliness always comes into play, but is there another news value present? One of the key questions about breaking news is this: Is it something that a significant number of people are talking about? Is it something that people want more information about? If the answer to either of those questions is yes, it is likely to qualify as breaking news.

Once the assessment is made that an item may qualify as breaking news, a second level of assessment requires the journalist to ask, "Who has the information I need? How can I get it?" Journalists should always be ready to talk with someone, even if it is the person sitting in the next seat and ask, "Where did you hear about that?"

Respond. Once a journalist has decided to treat information as breaking news, the goal is to gather and distribute as much information as possible as quickly as possible. A number of factors should come under consideration.

• availability of information

• means of distribution – news website, Twitter, Facebook?

• equipment (hardware) at hand

• nature of the information – is it finished or will it need to be updated?

In class

In considering deadline reporting, take another look at the four types of news stories that are produced on deadline at the beginning of this chapter. Go to your favorite news website and try to find an example of each. Read them carefully and try to analyze how the reporter produced the story.

A large crowd of baseball fans gathered outside the offices of the Washington Post in Washington, D.C., in October 1912 to watch the play-by-play results of the World Series on a Play-o-Graph, a large board that simulated a baseball diamond. The events of the game between the Boston Red Sox and the New York Giants came to the newspaper office by telephone. In the days before radio, television and the web, such scenes were common, particularly with a popular sport like baseball. The photo demonstrates that people have always wanted news as quickly as they could get it – and that they have been fascinated by the novelty of new technology.

2.3 Instructors: Preparing your students to cover breaking news

Instructors should begin preparing students for covering breaking news early in the course by doing some or all of the following:

Class discussions. Many students do not know how news organizations operate or even how they are structured. They do not know the role of editors, producers or news directors. A thorough discussion of the structure and procedure of a daily news organization should take place in the labs. Instructors may want to bring in (or call up) an example of a news story that was written on a deadline and talk about how that story was put together – what reporters and editors and producers did to get that story in shape so that it could be distributed.

Orientation to the web as a news medium. The web is a different type of medium from print or broadcast, even though it accepts many of the forms of news presentation of these traditional media. One of the main differences between the web and traditional media is its immediacy. A story can be posted to the website as soon as it is ready; there is no production time lag. A story can be updated in seconds. This characteristic drives a different dynamic for journalists – one that most students do not yet understand. This is journalism accelerated.

In-class exercises. Students can be oriented to the concepts of breaking news through in-class exercises. These can take a variety of forms, such as handing them a sheet of information about something that happened on campus (fictional) and giving them a very short deadline to produce a story. For instance, you might give them 15 minutes to produce a headline, summary and two or three paragraphs. There are many ways to do this (including guest speakers), but the point is that they need to respond very quickly to the information they have. (One exercise is to have them produce something with an initial set of facts and then to update that with more information after they have completed the first story.)

Out-of-class exercises. It is a very good idea for students to get a feel for breaking news by having them produce at least one (more is better) breaking news story before the class undertakes its breaking news week. Again, this could be done in a variety of ways, such as releasing the students from class and telling them they have until a certain time that night to send the instructor a story about something that has happened on campus that day.

Critiques. Both of the types of exercises above should produce fodder for thorough critiques and in-class discussions about how information is gathered, what kind of information is available and significant, the time it takes to write even a short story, the techniques that journalists use to produce daily (or hourly or minute-by-minute) news, and many other aspects of breaking news.

2.4 The UT experience

The following is a description of the some of the thoughts and experiences we have had at the University of Tennessee in having our JEM 230 Media Reporting course students cover breaking news:

Breaking news – its concepts and operations – is an important part of what we teach in JEM 230 (Media Reporting). Our students seem to know and understand little about the concept of breaking news or how it is produced. There is some tendency on their part to think that breaking news does not apply to them, even though they are journalism majors.

Because we produce our breaking news stories for the Tennessee Journalist (TNJN.com), an orientation toward web news coverage is particularly important. Within all of this, of course, must be a continued emphasis on good journalism – accurate, clearly written, precise and efficient reports. We are producing REAL news for a real news medium, one that on a normal semester day has between 1,500 and 2,000 (or more) readers.

Breaking news week

Each JEM 230 lab is assigned to cover breaking news on campus for a week during the middle of the semester. The students in the lab should act as a news team with the instructor in the role of managing editor or news director. (This role might be handed off to a student in the lab, but it would have to be someone who is very mature and very experienced.)

The instructor and the lab should go through the same kind of planning (budget meetings, story pitches, etc.) that a news organization would conduct during the week before the breaking news week. Firm guidelines, directions and expectations should be established for students. Scheduling of coverage may depend on the number of students in the lab, so that can be left to the individual lab instructor. Ideally, a student would be assigned to cover breaking news for at least two days during the week, particularly since the lab itself is probably not going to meet that week.

Deadlines are an important element of breaking news week, and those should be discussed so that students clearly understand them. Students also should be told what they are to produce – story length, photos, links, etc.

The instructor should also coordinate with the TNJN editors to make sure that those editors know what the class is doing, when they are doing it and what to expect in terms of stories. (The JEM 230 coordinator can help in this regard.) Not everything can be planned, of course. That is the point of breaking news. We don't know what will happen. It is the responsibility of the TNJN editors to keep in touch with the instructor and the students so that the news produced by the JEM 230 students can be posted in a timely fashion.

Following up

Once a JEM 230 lab has gone through its breaking news week, there should be a complete post mortem of what occurred. Getting the students to talk about what happened that week and what their experiences were will give instructors an opportunity to emphasize some of the concepts that we want to teach.

3. Tools of reporting

Journalists use four tools to present information: text, images, audio and video. Modern journalism requires that all journalists be adept in their use of each of these tools.

3.1 Writing

Writing is a vital part of the journalistic process, and we pay a great deal of attention to the forms and techniques of journalistic writing in the another book in this series.

But writing and reporting are intertwined, and as you begin to learn about information and reporting, you should also be learning about writing journalistically. In fact, your instructor may be covering these sections together, and doing makes a lot of sense.

Knowing what you have to write and the way you write it influences the information that you obtain to produce an article or report. For instance, most stories for print or the web require the inclusion of direct quotations from a live source. Consequently, in reporting on the story, the journalist will try to find someone who can provide that direct quotation.

In reporting for the web, it is important to include a list if that is possible and appropriate. Lists are easy for readers to see and comprehend quickly. So, the journalist writing for a web site will be on the lookout for some items that can be made into a list.

Principles of clear, effective writing

You've probably had a newswriting course already or maybe you have had some news writing experience. Whatever your background, you undoubtedly know that writing is an essential part of the reporting process. So, here are a few tips to remind you about some of the techniques of writing that journalists use.

Use short words rather than long ones.

> The reporter's job is to select information and translate it into language that most people will understand. The reporter generally prefers shorter words to longer one ("use" as opposed to "facilitate") because they are more efficient and more people are likely to understand them.

Prefer familiar words over unfamiliar ones.

Makes sense, doesn't it? Write in the language that your readers will understand. Don't try to dazzle them with all of the words that you know.

Be precise.

Be sure that each word conveys its precise meaning. Use your dictionary and thesaurus. Make sure you know the difference between words that may be pronounced the same but have different spellings. You will save yourself some embarrassment.

Use strong verbs, and prefer active over passive voice.

The one secret that professional writers always share is that verbs -- strong, accurate, descriptive verbs -- carry much more informational weight than adjectives or adverbs. When you write something, look at the verbs that you are using. If your writing is filled with linking verbs (was, is, were, etc.), try to find some strong, descriptive verbs to substitute for them.

Watch use of qualifying words and phrases.

Check your adjectives, adverbs and prepositional phrases. Are they needed? Prefer the use of nouns and verbs to adjectives and adverbs.

Use short sentences.

Try not to average more than 20 words per sentence.

Vary sentence length.

Balance long sentences with short ones. Monotony in sentence length puts the reader to sleep.

Be straightforward.

Rambling sentences, filled with qualifying clauses, cause the reader to lose the train of thought. You should take the most direct route between subject, verb and object.

Avoid wordiness, jargon, pompous phrases and generalities.

These things can be killers to good writing. The only time you should take pride in your writing is when it conveys the information and ideas that you want to convey in a simple and straightforward manner.

Use restraint.

Sound facts speak for themselves. An understatement is often more effective than flamboyant words and phrases.

Revise.

Read and reread and then revise and rewrite until you have achieved clarity. Make revision a part of the writing process, not just something you do when you think about it. Never turn in a first draft.

Use transitions.

Weave the copy into a coherent whole by using transitional words, phrases and paragraphs. Avoid abrupt shifts from one topic to another in a story.

Read your story aloud.

You would be surprised at how quickly bad writing is revealed when you read something aloud. If you stumble or get confused when reading a passage aloud, it needs to be rewritten. If you can't read a sentence in one normal breath, it's too long.

As you learn about journalistic information, pay attention to the kind of information you will need and the form that it should take so that it can be included in your reports.

Video

Watch a video of journalism professor Ed Caudill as he explains the history of newswriting on Vimeo at **https://vimeo.com/14513323**

3.2 Charts and maps

A reporter wrote the following for her story:

Attendance by City Council members varies a good deal. A check of the minutes for all of last year's meetings reveals that only Alvin Barkley had perfect attendance at all of the regularly scheduled meeting (25) and at all of the called meetings (13). The council member who attended the fewest meetings was Thomas Fairbanks, who was at only 15 of the regular meetings and five of the called meetings. Among the others, Charlene Dawes attended the most of the regular meetings (24) and was at all 13 of the called meetings. Thomas Marshall, like Fairbanks, attended only five of the called meetings, but he was at 19 of the regular meetings. John Garner was at 20 of the regular meetings and 12 of the called meetings. Henrietta Wallace was at 19 of the regular meetings and 10 of the called meetings, while Billie Jean Wheeler was at 16 of the regular meetings and 11 of the called meetings.

Or, she could have simply constructed the following chart:

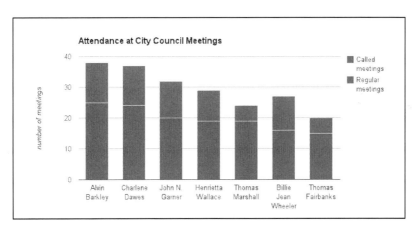

Which do you think her readers would have appreciated more -- the paragraph or the chart?

Which would have gained their attention?

Which would they have understood more quickly?

What do you learn from the chart that you don't get from the paragraph?

Once the data was gathered, the chart took less than five minutes to construct. Was that a worthwhile use of the reporter's time?

Many journalists and readers would say yes to that last question. A well-constructed chart can gain the reader's attention and can inform the reader more quickly that text. In addition, readers can infer information from a chart that the journalist might not have the knowledge or inclination to point out in the text. And, some research shows that information in charts in more credible to some readers than information in text.

Characteristics of chart-based graphics

Chart-based graphics are graphics that present numerical information in a non-text form, usually in one of the standard chart forms. These forms are likely to be proportional representations of the numbers themselves. These are what many people refer to when they talk about informational graphics.

Good chart-based graphics should exhibit the following characteristics:

Simplicity. Graphics can be complex, but their appearance should be uncluttered. One of the criticisms of many graphics is that they are "chartoons" — that is, they have too many little figures and drawings that do not add to the reader's understanding of the information in the graphic. A graphic should contain the minimum items necessary for understanding the information and the maximum items for good appearance.

Consistency. Websites and publications often develop a graphics style just as they adopt a writing style. This style includes rules about what kind of type is used, when color is appropriate, how information is attributed, and a variety of other matters. Like style rules for writing, these rules help both the staff in producing graphics and the reader in understanding them.

Attribution. Information in graphics should be attributed, just as information in news stories should be attributed. As with other information in a publication, sometimes the source is obvious and does not need to be specified. In other cases, attribution is vital to the understanding of a graphic.

Headlines. Oddly enough, one of the most difficult things about producing an informational graphic is writing its headline. Headlines for graphics do not have to follow the rules of headlines for articles; in most publications, they can simply be labels. They need to identify the central idea of the graphic, however, and this is difficult to do in just a few words. One approach many graphic journalists use to writing a headline for a graphic is to write it before the graphic is built. Doing that gives them the central idea to keep in mind while producing the graphic.

Types of charts that present numerical data

Most mass media publications use three types of chart-based graphics: the bar chart, the line chart, and the pie chart. (There are other types of charts for presenting numerical information such as the scattergraph, but these are not commonly found in the mass media.) Each type of chart is best used for presenting certain types of information and is inappropriate for other types of information. Editors need to understand what charts are appropriate for what types of information.

Making charts with Google spreadsheets

Watch this video at https://vimeo.com/56532388 to learn the simple process of making am interactive chart for your publication or website with Google spreadsheets.

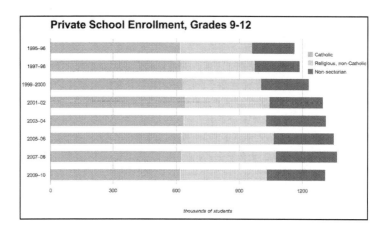

Private School Enrollment, Grades 9-12

Catholic
Religious, non-Catholic
Non-sectarian

thousands of students

Bar charts. The bar chart (above) is the most popular type of chart because it is easy to set up, and it can be used in many ways. The bar chart uses thick lines or rectangles to present its information. These rectangles represent the amounts or values in the data presented in the chart. There are technically two types of bar charts. One uses the namebar chart and refers to charts in which the bars run horizontally. The column chart refers to bar charts in which the bars run vertically. Column charts are more commonly used when time is an element in the data, but that is not a strict rule.

The two major lines in a bar chart are the horizontal axis, known as the x-axis, and the vertical axis, known as the y-axis. Both should have clearly defined starting points so that the information in the chart is not distorted, particularly the axis that represents the amounts in the graph.

One of the reasons a bar chart is so popular is that it can show both amounts and relationships. It can also show a change in amounts and relationships over time. The chart above demonstrates the bar chart's ability to show relationships, particularly when there is a large amount of data. From a brief look at this chart, the reader knows how these colleges compare to one another as well as something about each school.

So, here's what important about a bar chart:

•*A bar chart is good for showing a single set of data, or — to a limited extent — multiple sets of data.*

• *A bar chart allows you to compare pieces or sets of data easily.*

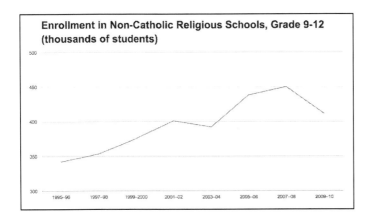

**Enrollment in Non-Catholic Religious Schools, Grade 9-12
(thousands of students)**

Line charts. Whereas the bar chart may show change over time, the line chart (above) must show change over time -- or trends. It can also show a change in relationships over time. In some instances, it is preferable to the bar chart because it is cleaner and easier to decipher.

The line chart uses a line or set of lines to represent amounts or values. One of the standard conventions of the line chart is that the x-axis represents the time element and the y-axis represents the amounts or quantities being represented.

Line charts can use more than one line to show not only how one item has changed but the relationship of changes of several items. Data points can be represented by different shapes for each item. The danger with multiple line charts is that too many lines can be confusing to the reader. Graphic journalists should avoid putting more than three lines in a line chart.

Here's what's important about line charts:

• *A line chart shows change over time.*

• *Data amounts are always shown on the Y-axis (vertical).*

• *Time is always shown on the X-axis (horizontal).*

• *Any use of a line chart to show something other than change over time is incorrect.*

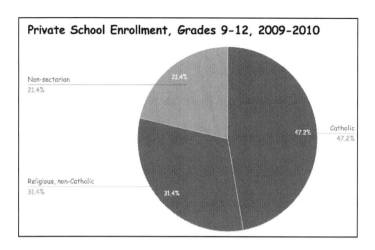

Private School Enrollment, Grades 9-12, 2009-2010

Non-sectarian
21.4%

21.4%

Catholic
47.2%

47.2%

Religious, non-Catholic
31.4%

31.4%

Pie charts. The pie chart (above) is another popular means of showing data, but its use is specialized. A pie chart should show how an entity or item is divided up, and the divisions are most commonly expressed in percentages that add up to 100 percent. Figures also may be used to identify the parts of a pie chart, but it is important that the creator of a pie chart keep the concept of percentages in mind.

Despite the strict limits of the kind of data that can be shown in a pie chart, this type of chart can be used in a variety of ways. A pie chart can show only one set of data at a time, but several charts can be used together to help compare sets of data.

Here's what's important about pie charts:

• *A pie chart should be used only to show parts of a whole.*

• *Time is not an element in pie chart data.*

• *Data in a pie chart usually are expressed as percentages, and those percentages must add up to 100.*

If you are really interested in charts and graphs and in displaying numerical information correctly, you should take a look at the books of Edward Tufte, beginning with *The Visual Display of Quantitative Information.* They are amazing and absorbing books that are beautifully designed and produced.

Maps

Where are you?

Where is the story?

A map can tell you.

One of the most common and useful graphic devices in today's mass media is the map. Maps are quick and easy to use. They provide readers with important information that can be used to help explain events and put them in physical context. In addition, they help to educate a public that many have tagged as geographically illiterate.

Certain conventions should be followed in using maps. First and foremost, a map should always be proportional to the geographic area that it represents; that is, it should be "to scale." Let's say that a country is 2,000 miles long from north to south and 1,000 miles long from east to west. The longitude (north to south) to latitude (east to west) scale is 2 to 1. Any map that represents that area should have the north-south line twice the distance of the east-west line.

Another important convention of maps is that the northern part of the area represented is always at the top of the map. This northern orientation dates from ancient times and is one of the assumptions that most people make when they look at a map.

A third convention of maps is that they include a distance scale, usually somewhere close to the bottom of the map. Not every map needs a distance scale because sometimes such a scale is irrelevant. On those maps where the area is likely to be unfamiliar to the reader, distance scales are extremely helpful. A distance scale usually consists of two parts: a line that is marked off to indicate units of a distance on the map; and text that tells what the scale is, such as "1 inch = 5 miles."

Many maps in newspapers or magazines appear with insets— smaller maps that show a larger area that includes the area shown in the map. For instance, a map of Great Britain might include an inset of Western Europe to show where or how large Great Britain is in relation to other countries.

The news media put maps to three basic uses with which you should be familiar:

Symbols. The shapes of many states and countries are well known and are excellent graphic devices. They are particularly useful when an article is divided up as a series of reports on different states or countries (or, on a more local level, counties). While such use does not require that these maps have a distance scale, they should follow the conventions of being proportionally scaled and having the north at the top.

Location. Using maps to indicate the location of events is what we think of as the most common and logical use of maps. Here, all of the conventions of map usage should come into consideration.

These maps may be enhanced by a number of devices. Cities, towns and other locations can be identified. A map may also include buildings or other sites that would help the reader get the point of the map. Hills, valleys, mountains, rivers, forests and other topographical factors can be included on a map with drawings or shadings.

Maps may serve as backgrounds for other information that journalists want to convey to their readers. For instance, to give readers a better sense of the story about a trip by the pope, a publication might include a map with text and arrows pointing to the different locations the pope will visit and the dates on his schedule.

Location maps may not always have to be of areas that we think of as geographic locations. For instance, the floor plan of a house or other building can be treated as a map if it helps readers understand something about an article. In the general sense, maps are a way of looking down on something and seeing it as a whole rather than seeing part of it from the limits of ground level. Such a bird's eye view can be revealing and insightful.

Data. A data map places numerical data on geographic locations in a way that will produce relevant information about the data. Data maps can aid in our understanding of the data and the areas in which it occurs. Data maps also allow readers to view large amounts of information at a single sighting in an orderly and logical way.

Data maps take time and effort to produce, and they should be created with great care. Data maps that are not carefully thought out can allow viewers to reach superficial or incorrect conclusions. Creators of data maps should be particularly careful that the data they have is, in fact, related to geographic location rather than being distributed randomly.

Data map controversy

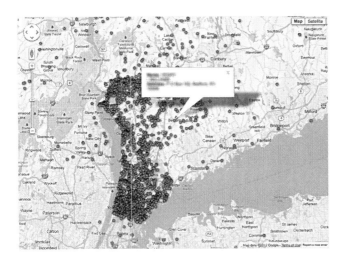

This data map sparked great controversy in late December 2012. Published by **lohud.com,** the website of the Journal News in Westchester County, N.Y., it shows the households in the county for which pistol permits had been issued in the previous five years. It gives the names and addresses of those households. The information was taken from county public records, but many people said the map was an invasion of privacy. Editors countered, saying they wanted to alert readers to the fact that their neighbors might have a gun. Westchester County is just a few miles from Sandy Hook, Conn., where two weeks before then, 20 children and eight adults had been murdered while attending school. What do you think about this map and its publication?

Links: The story: The gun owner next door: What you don't know about the weapons in your neighborhood, **http://lohud.us/UYOtgp.** Map: Where are the gun permits in your neighborhood? **http://lohud.us/UiMaqQ.** (Note: The name and address on this map have been deliberately blurred.)

Sidebar:

Statistical terms used in research studies: a primer for journalists

When assessing academic studies, reporters are often confronted by pages not only full of numbers, but also loaded with concepts such as "selection bias," "p-value" and "statistical inference."

Statistics courses are available at most universities, of course, but are often viewed by journalism students as something to be taken, passed and quickly forgotten. However, for working reporters it is imperative to do more than just read study abstracts; understanding the methods and concepts that underpin academic studies is essential to being able to judge the merits of a particular piece of research.

Further, the emerging field of data journalism requires that reporters bring more analytical rigor to the increasingly large amounts of numbers, figures and data they use. Understanding some of the academic theory behind statistics can help ensure that rigor.

Most studies attempt to establish a correlation between two variables — for example, how community education levels might be "associated with" (a phrase often used by academics) crime rates. But detecting such a relationship is only a first step; the ultimate goal is to determine causation: that one of the two variables drives the other. There is a time-honored phrase to keep in mind: "Correlation is not causation." (This can be usefully amended to "correlation is not necessarily causation," as the nature of the relationship needs to be determined.)

Another key distinction to keep in mind is that studies can either explore observed data (descriptive statistics) or use observed data to predict what is true of areas beyond the data (inferential statistics). The statement "From 2000 to 2005, 70% of the land cleared in the Amazon and recorded in Brazilian government data was transformed into pasture" is a descriptive statistic; "Receiving your college degree increases your lifetime earnings by 50%" is an inferential statistic.

Here are some other basic statistical concepts that journalism students and working journalists should be familiar with:

• A **sample** is a portion of an entire population. Inferential statistics seek to make predictions about a population based on the results observed in a sample of that population.

• There are two primary types of population samples: **random and stratified**. For a random sample, study subjects are chosen completely by chance, while a stratified sample is constructed to reflect the characteristics of the population at large (gender, age or ethnicity, for example).

• Attempting to extend the results of a sample to a population is called **generalization**. This can be done only when the sample is truly representative of the entire population.

• Generalizing results from a sample to the population must take into account sample variation. Even if the sample selected is completely random, there is still a degree of variance within the population that will require your results from within a sample to include a margin of error. For example, the results of a poll of likely voters could give the margin of error in percentage points: "47% of those polled said they would vote for the measure, with a margin of error of 3 percentage points." Thus, if the actual percentage voting for the measure was as low as 44% or as high as 50%, this result would be consistent with the poll.

• The greater the sample size, the more representative it tends to be of a population as a whole. Thus the **margin of error** falls and the confidence level rises.

• Most studies explore the relationship between two variables — for example, that prenatal exposure to pesticides is associated with lower birthweight. This is called the alternative hypothesis. Well-designed studies seek to disprove the null hypothesis — in this case, that prenatal pesticide exposure is not associated with lower birthweight.

• **Significance tests** of the study's results determine the probability that the null hypothesis is invalid; the p-value indicates how much evidence there is. If the p-value is 0.05, there is a 95% probability that the null hypothesis is invalid; if the p-value is 0.01, there is a 99% probability.

• The other threat to a sample's validity is the notion of **bias**.

Bias comes in many forms but most common bias is based on the selection of subjects. For example, if subjects self-select into a sample group, then the results are no longer externally valid, as the type of person who wants to be in a study is not necessarily similar to the population that we are seeking to draw inference about.

• When two variables move together, they are said to be **correlated**. Positive correlation means that as one variable rises or falls, the other does as well — caloric intake and weight, for example. Negative correlation indicates that two variables move in opposite directions — say, vehicle speed and travel time. So if a scholar writes "Income is negatively correlated with poverty rates," what he or she means is that as income rises, poverty rates fall.

• **Elasticity**, a term frequently used in economics studies, measures how much a change in one variable affects another. For example, if the price of vegetables rises 10% and consumers respond by cutting back purchases by 10%, the expenditure elasticity is 1.0 — the increase in price equals the drop in consumption. But if purchases fall by 15%, the elasticity is 1.5, and consumers are said to be "price sensitive" for that item. If consumption were to fall only 5%, the elasticity is 0.5 and consumers are "price insensitive" — a rise in price of a certain amount doesn't reduce purchases to the same degree.

• **Regression analysis** is a way to determine if there is or isn't a correlation between two variables and how strong any correlation may be. At its most basic, this involves plotting data points on a X/Y axis (in our example, community education levels and crime rates) looking for the average causal effect. This means looking at how the graph's dots are distributed and establishing a trend line. Again, correlation isn't necessarily causation.

• **Standard deviation** provides insight into how much variation there is within a group of values. It measures the deviation (difference) from the group's mean (average).

• Be careful to distinguish the following terms as you interpret results: **Average, mean and median**. The first two terms are synonymous, and refer to the average value of a group of numbers. Add up all the figures, divide by the number of values, and that's the average or mean. A median, on the other hand, is the central value, and can be useful if there's an extremely high or low value in a collection of values — say, Bill Gates's salary in a list of people's incomes. (For more information, read "Math for Journalists" or go to one of the "related resources" at right.)

- In descriptive statistics, quantiles can be used to divide data into equal-sized subsets. For example, dividing a list of individuals sorted by height into two parts — the tallest and the shortest — results in two quantiles, with the median height value as the dividing line. Quartiles separate data set into four equal-sized groups, deciles into 10 groups, and so forth. Individual items can be described as being "in the upper decile," meaning the group with the largest values, meaning that they are higher than 90% of those in the dataset.

- **Causation** is when change in one variable alters another. For example, air temperature and sunlight are correlated (when the sun is up, temperatures rise), but causation flows in only one direction. This is also known as cause and effect.

- When causation has been established, the factor that drives change (in the above example, sunlight) is the independent variable. The variable that is driven is the dependent variable.

- While causation is sometimes easy to prove, frequently it can often be difficult because of confounding variables (unknown factors that affect the two variables being studied). Studies require well-designed and executed experiments to ensure that the results are reliable.

There are a number of free online statistics tutorials available, including one from Stat Trek and another from Experiment Resources. Stat Trek also offer a glossary that provides definitions of common statistical terms. Another useful resource is "Harnessing the Power of Statistics," a chapter in The New Precision Journalism.

Note that understanding statistical terms isn't a license to freely salt your stories with them. Always work to present studies' key findings in clear, jargon-free language. You'll be doing a service not only for your readers, but also for the researchers.

- See more at:
http://journalistsresource.org/skills/research/statistics-for-journalists#sthash.sXpYvgN2.dpuf

3.3 Photojournalism

The invention of photography in the 1830s changed the way people looked at their world and the way that ideas are shared and imprinted on our brains.

This invention had a profound effect on the way journalism is produced.

The development of photography in the 1830s was one of the most profound changes that has affected the way we view the world.

Photography brings to life people, places, events and other things that we would otherwise have trouble understanding. It has given us a common set of images with which to understand the environment that we do not personally experience.

Photographs – still images – are particularly effective in making a lasting impression on our brains. More than video – moving pictures – photographs allow us to reduce a person, place, event or subject to a manageable set of information that we can carry with us. The "pictures in our heads" have a great deal to do with the way we comprehend and interpret the things in our larger world.

For all of these reasons, photography is an important part of journalism. It, along with the words that we use, is a vital part of telling the story we have to tell. Photography gives the audience for journalism another dimension of information that they cannot get with words. It often gives life and form to the words that journalists use. It helps to entertain the audience as well as to deepen their understanding of the information in a story.

Photography is a way of impressing a story onto the brain of a reader.

Photojournalism became a possibility for journalism soon after the invention of photography in the 1830s. Cameras became a widely popular social phenomenon in the 1840s because they were new and people could have fun with them. The power of the photographic image was evident to journalists, but technology stymied its use. Newspapers and magazines were unable to reproduce photographs on their presses for many years, thus limiting the advance of photojournalism.

One of the first great photojournalists was Matthew Brady, a New York portrait photographer who traveled to many of the battlefields of the American Civil War in the 1860s to record what had happened there. Brady's images brought home to people who had stayed behind the starkness and horrors of war and helped change the way that people thought about war itself.

But photojournalism during the last part of the 19th century was not an easy thing to accomplish. The equipment required to take a picture was heavy, fragile and unreliable. Developing pictures from the film that had to be used was difficult and tedious. And even when the picture was taken and developed, there was no quick way of printing and distributing it widely because printing presses were developed to use type, not pictures.

These technical problems were gradually mitigated with the development of lighter and more portable cameras (although they were still massive machines compared to the tiny, hand-held cameras we have today). Film and the development process became more standardized, but it was never a particularly easy thing to get a print from film. Most importantly, the half-toning process for printing pictures allowed printers a quick way of getting sharp, clear and detailed images onto presses so they could be widely distributed.

By the middle of the 20th century, photography was an integral and important part of the journalistic process.

Because film photography and development had evolved into a highly precise and technical process, and because the skills to do this were ones that photographers had to hone over many years, photojournalists were slowed to accept digital photography when it became widely available in the 1990s. Digital photography bypassed film and the development process (sometimes called "wet photography") by recording photos onto electronic disks and then using computers and software to produce the pictures.

Digital photography, from its beginnings, was definitely faster, and as quality equipment became much cheaper, it replaced film photography as the standard operating process for photojournalism. With today's cameras used in conjunction with the web, photos can be taken and transmitted around the world in a matter of seconds, where that process once took days or even weeks.

The digital revolution in photojournalism ushered in a more profound change in journalism and made it possible to take and produce pictures quickly. It brought photography within the reach of every journalist. While some people still consider themselves photojournalists, all journalists must consider themselves photographers. Photography should be a part of every story that every journalists covers.

That means:

- All journalists should understand the basics of good picture taking.
- Journalists should carry a camera and be familiar with its technical aspects.
- Journalists should understand the software for editing photographs and should be very familiar with the process of preparing and uploading photos to the web.
- Most importantly, journalists must integrate photography into their thinking about every story they cover.

Ask yourself:

Look at the photographs in the slideshow in this module. Each of the five photos will appear for 10 seconds. Which one do you remember? Describe it in as much detail as you can.

Why do you remember it?

Video

Dr. Michael Martinez of the University of Tennessee talks about what a photojournalism needs to think about in approaching photo assignments and stories. Watch the video:
https://vimeo.com/52784417

3.4 Audio journalism

Audio journalism is reporting news and information with sound. Doing this was once the exclusive domain of radio, and radio was once the dominant news medium.

Before and during World War II, radio developed into the speedy, reliable news source that people around the world came to depend on. A chief figure in this development was Edward R. Murrow, whose reports from London during the early days of World War II seemed to place listeners in the midst of the bombing of that city.

Murrow's style of reporting — accurate and detached but also personal and conversational — resonates today as much as it did then. Sound is a compelling medium, and Murrow was one of its early pioneers. (For an example of Murrow's reporting, go to http://archive.org/details/murrow_in_london_1942 .)

The development of television after World War II put a quick end to radio's dominance. Radio became a medium for music but not for news, and by the late 1960s, there simply wasn't very much radio news.

Except for National Public Radio and the efforts of a few isolated individuals and organizations, radio journalism for more than 50 years has been under-developed. Even where radio journalism is good — and on NPR it can be very good — it is still confined to the medium and restricted by time, programming constraints and geography.

The emergence of the web as a dominant news medium has freed radio journalism — what we can more properly call audio journalism — from those restraints.

The advantages of learning and using audio as a reporting tool are legion:

• It is easy to produce. The equipment necessary for recording can fit into your shirt pocket. The software (Audacity is among the best) is simple and can be mastered quickly.

• Sound can take a story beyond text (just as pictures can). Audio within a news story gives readers/listeners an added dimension that nothing else can duplicate.

• Audio literally gives sources a "voice." By using sound rather than text, their words, tones and inflections can be heard, not just described. Ambient sound can give these voices added context that increases the richness of the reporting.

• Sound allows listeners to "see" with the best lens of all, the mind. Sounds fire the imagination and allow listeners to draw their own pictures. This quality is particularly valuable and powerful in this age of video and television.

• The idea of audio journalism at this point is largely unexplored. That means that the people who get into it now have an opportunity to define the form. The next generation can experiment and be creative without having the burdens of "tradition" or the concept of "best practices."

• Audio is a presentation form that allows the audience to multitask. Reading text and watching video demand the full attention of the visitor. Audio lets the audience do something else in addition to taking in the information. As the demand for consumer time increases, this will continue to be an important consideration for the web journalist.

Finally, audio journalism is important because it is the dominant form of information distribution on The Next Big Thing in Journalism: mobile journalism. Despite all the current attention to texting, web site scaling and video on cellphones and hand-held devices, people generally use these devices to talk and to receive sound, either from other talkers or from audio producers.

Edward R. Murrow (right) was one of the great figures in the development of broadcast news. His reports from London during World War II set many of the standards for broadcast journalism.

All of these are compelling reasons why we to pay serious attention to the concept and forms of audio journalism. Sound can be an exciting tool to work with as reporters and a valuable means of presenting information for our audience.

Writing for audio

Broadcast journalists of previous times talked about the Four Cs of broadcast writing — correctness, clarity, conciseness and color.

These four Cs still serve as a good framework for learning writing styles.

Accuracy, correctness, for any journalist is the number one goal.

The first commitment of the broadcast journalist is to correctness, or accuracy. Everything a broadcast journalist does must contribute to the telling of an accurate story. Even though the broadcast journalist must observe some strict rules about how stories are written, these rules should contribute to, not prevent, an accurate account of an event.

Clarity is one of the most admirable characteristics of good broadcast writing. Good broadcast writers employ clear, precise language that contains no ambiguity.

Clarity is an absolute requirement for broadcast writing. Listeners and viewers cannot go back and re-hear a news broadcast as they might be able to read a newspaper account more than once. They must understand what is said the first time. Broadcast writers achieve this kind of clarity by using simple sentences and familiar words, by avoiding the use of pronouns and repeating proper nouns if necessary and by keeping the subject close to the verb in their sentences. Most of all, however, they achieve clarity by thoroughly knowing and understanding their subject.

A conversational style is a plus for writing for broadcasting.

Even the clearest, simplest newspaper style tends to sound stilted when it is read aloud. Broadcast writing must sound more conversational because people will be reading it aloud. Broadcast news should be written for the ear, not the eye. The writer should keep in mind that someone is going to say the words and others will listen to them.

This casual or conversational style, however, does not give the writer freedom to break the rules of grammar, to use slang or off-color phrasing or to use language that might be offensive to listeners. As with all writing, the broadcast writer should try to focus attention on the content of the writing and not the writing itself. Nor is casual–sounding prose particularly easy to produce. It takes a finely-honed ear for the language and a conciseness that we do not normally apply to writing.

Another characteristic of writing for broadcast is the emphasis on the immediate. While past tense verbs are preferred in the print media, broadcasters use the present tense as much as possible. A newspaper or Web site story might begin something like this:

Research indicates dangers from antacids

> *SAN FRANCISCO – Antacids fail to protect anti-arthritis drug users from serious internal bleeding and may even increase that risk because they mask symptoms, according to two new studies.*
>
> *The findings could affect an estimated 6 million Americans who use arthritis drugs and routinely take antacids to prevent stomach discomfort.*

But a broadcast story on the same topic might go like this:

> *If you're one of the six million people who take anti-arthritis drugs, you need to be careful about the antacid drugs that you may be also taking.*
>
> *Doctors at Stanford University have found that antacids do not protect users from serious internal bleeding that their anti-arthritis drugs may cause. In fact, they may mask some of the symptoms of internal bleeding, and that could be harmful to the patient.*

Another way of emphasizing the immediate is to omit the time element in the news story and assume that everything has happened close to the time of the broadcast. In the example above, the broadcast version has no time element since it would probably be heard on the day the doctors made that statement. The elimination of the time element cannot occur in every story. Sometimes the time element is important and must be mentioned.

Conciseness – writing that is loaded with words that deliver information to the reader – is a major part of learning to write for broadcasting.

The tight phrasing that characterizes broadcast writing is one of its chief assets and one of the most difficult qualities for a beginning writer to achieve. Because time is so short, the broadcaster cannot waste words. The broadcaster must work constantly to simplify and condense.

There are a number of techniques for achieving this conciseness. One technique is the elimination of all but the most necessary adjectives and adverbs. Broadcasters know that their stories are built on nouns and verbs, the strongest words in the language. They avoid using the passive voice. Instead they rely on strong, active verbs that will allow the listener to form a picture of the story.

Another technique of broadcast writing is the use of short, simple sentences. Broadcasters do not need the variety of length and type of sentences that print journalists need to make their copy interesting. Broadcasters can more readily fire information at their readers like bullets in short, simple sentences.

One broadcaster put it this way: The best broadcast sentences are

Subject > verb > predicate > period.

The fourth C — color — refers to writing that allows the listener to paint a picture of the story or event being reported. This picture can be achieved in a variety of ways, such as the inclusion of pertinent and insightful details in the story or allowing the personality of the writer or news reader to come through in a story. The nature of the broadcast medium allows for humor and human interest to inject itself into many stories.

Audio journalism ethics

The audio reporter must abide by the same ethical standards of any other journalist. The audio journalist has the same goal: to provide accurate, significant and interesting information in an accurate context to an audience. Therefore, it is incumbent on the audio journalist to:

• tell the truth, both about the story and the process of reporting

• make sure the audience knows enough to evaluate the information properly

Audio journalists strive for accuracy, clarity, significance and the interesting in telling their stories – and in that order.

In addition, audio journalists must:

- always have permission (explicit or implied) to record someone's voice
- give equal weight (not necessarily time) to opposing points of view
- attempt to give voice to those who aren't usually heard

Audio journalism is more than information via sound. It is also a matter of

• **sequence.** Order is important, particularly when people are speaking. Most of the time you will want to preserve that order. When you decide to change the order of people's words or sentence, be sure that the change is fair and accurate.

• **tone.** How people sound is important. Are they happy, sad, surprised, impressed, or what? If someone exhibits some emotion in an interview, make sure that emotion is convey accurately. For instance, a person who has lost a loved one to some accident may make a wry comment just to relieve the tension. Don't use that if it makes the person sound heartless or cold.

• **ambience** (context of the sound). Context in audio reporting is vitally important. Sounds report the conditions under which people talk. The sounds should add to the listener's understanding and impressions, but those impressions must be accurately derived.

All of these have an impact on the way the story is told and the impression that it leaves on the listener.

The editing process

It is easier than ever to record and edit audio. Recorders today are small and powerful. Editing software makes manipulating the audio a quick and almost painless process. An audio journalist can do all sorts of things with a story – and can do them quickly – that radio journalists of previous days could not do.

So, here are some dos and don'ts:

• Remove noise that distracts and doesn't add to a story.

• Remove sounds of an interviewee that do not present information about his character or demeanor. For instance, most of the time "uhs"s, grunts and other noises can be safely deleted.

• Rarely, if ever, should you edit out single words.

• Delete repetitions and reiterations (most of the time).

• Consider deleting subordinate clauses.

• Don't coach an interviewee. Do not tell an interview what to say or give the person a script. Especially a script. If a person is reading something you can tell.

• Do not edit so that an interviewee sounds as if he or she is answering one question when the person is answering something else.

• You may remove whole sentences if they are extraneous, but take some care about that. The concept of sequence is important (above).

• Do not insert sounds that give a false impression to the listener.

• When you are interviewing, learn to be silent. Nod if you must, but do not utter any sounds.

• Do not interrupt an interviewee, and if you do, think hard before putting that interruption in the story you produce. In other words, try to stay out of the story.

• Remember that most of a recorded interview is likely to be cut. Make sure that the part that is left tells an accurate and fair story.

• Avoid "butt-cuts" – running two interviews together or interweaving them so that it appears that the two people are having a conversation.

• Be very careful not to leave the listener with a mistaken impression about you. For instance, don't edit something to indicate you were there when you weren't.

• Don't use sounds you didn't record yourself or you didn't record at the scene to make it seem like they were recorded at the scene. Mary McGuire:

> *For example, if you interview a carpenter but fail to record the sound of him at work in his workshop, you can't just record yourself using a hammer at home later and pretend, in your report, that it is the sound of the carpenter at work.*

• Use music sparingly.

3.5 Video journalism

Every story begins with an idea.

The idea then coalesces into something smaller and more practical. Something doable.

At some point in the process – sooner is better than later – the idea is condensed into a single sentence, so that if someone asked you, "What story are you working on right now?" you could tell that person in a single sentence and without hesitating.

If you can do that, chances are your idea is a good one and you will be able to produce a good video story.

If your story idea is still at the stage that you take several sentences to explain it, chances are you are not going to be able to produce it easily or coherently. Or that you are going to spend a lot of time doing things that are not necessary. Or both.

So, Rule Number One: Get the story idea together.

Rule Number One-A: Keep it simple.

Once you get the idea (one sentence – no more), then start asking the journalistic questions:

• Who. Who is involved in the story? What one or two people do I need to talk to? Can I get to them? Will they talk to me?

• What. What is the central piece of action or the central idea – the one thing around which the story is centered? Can I get a picture of it? Better yet, can I shoot video of it? How can I capture that with a video camera?

• Where. The location of the story is of prime importance. As a video journalist, you are going to have to go there. It's not likely that it will come to you. So, you ask: Can I get there? Can I take a camera? Is it a place where I can shoot video so that it will mean something to the people who watch the story?

• When. What is the time element of this story? Is it an event? Or is it an idea? Will it be gone tomorrow, or can the story wait for a day or a week? The last question does not mean you should consider procrastinating. It simply helps you with your planning.

When you get answers to those questions, you are beginning to think like a journalist.

But you are just beginning.

Now you should forming an outline for the story – a mental storyboard. You make some phone calls or send some emails. (If you are working on a story that will be broadcast that day, you make phone calls. Email – even texting – is too slow.) You ask people for information. You begin gathering facts, information, impressions. You get an idea of where the story is headed based on what you find out. Sometimes, your original central idea is confirmed. Sometimes it isn't. You have to adjust.

As the story begins to take shape in your head, you consider what you need to be telling and what you can show: interviews, action scenes, still pictures, pan shots, etc.

You set up interviews, and you go to where the sources are. You go to the scene of the event or story idea, if there is one. You are constantly thinking – constantly asking yourself: How can I tell this story? What do I need – an interview with Person A, a shot of Place B, etc.

Finally, when you have shot the video you think you need, you sit down to write. Unless it's breaking news and you're covering the event live, your story won't really come together until you have written it. And without good writing, your story won't be worth watching.

So you think about the arc of the story – the introduction, what bits go in the middle, the way it ends. What is the video that you want to use? Does it need an intro? Does it need a voice over? Are all these things related to the central idea of the story as you first defined it or as you adjusted it during your reporting?

Does the story hang together? Does the video support the writing?

Can the way you're telling the story be understood by a viewer who knows little or nothing about the story? Is it clear from the very beginning to the very end?

These are hard questions, but they are the ones the good video journalist asks again and again throughout the time that the story is being produced, all the while working under two extraordinarily difficult strictures:

Get it right.

Keep it simple.

Shooting the video

The camera does not speak. It does not tell the story. It is held, aimed, pointed, positioned.

The person holding the camera – the videographer is the professional term – is the story-teller.

The story is in the head of the journalist, who in many cases is the videographer as well as the writer and producer. The camera is simply the tool the journalist/videographer uses to get the story to the viewer.

How does that happen?

Here are some basic things that everyone who uses a video camera should know:

• **Plan and think.** The most important tool the video journalist has is not a camera. It's the brain. As much as possible, video journalists should find out what information they can about the story they are shooting, who's involved, where it's located and what will happen. They should know before they arrive on the scene the people they want to talk with and the kinds of shots they want to make.

In addition, they should also size up a situation quickly, hold the camera up and shoot the interesting things that happen right in front of them. Video journalists should shoot efficiently, but they should err on the side of having too much video rather than too little.

• **Framing.** The concept of framing simply means understanding what will look good when you turn the camera on and what won't. One of the rules of framing is to "fill the frame." That is, when you are shooting, you should not have much "margin" around the subject, if any at all. Generally, the closer you are to the subject, the better your shots and your framing will be. Another concept of framing is to apply the rule of thirds to the video camera. The rule of thirds is an imaginary set of horizontal lines that divide what you see in the viewfinder into three equal parts and an imaginary set of vital lines that do the same thing. Taken together, the picture is divided into nine parts. Seeing the picture divided like this helps in a number of ways. For one, if the picture is of someone's face, the person's eyes should be along the top horizontal line. Getting a center of interest at one of the four points where the lines intersect is also a useful technique.

Head room is another term you will hear in a discussion of framing. This refers to the space in a head shot between the top of the head and the top of the picture. Generally, there should be some space for head room, but sometimes filling the picture with the head – or even cutting off the top of the head – may be appropriate for the story.

• **Holding the camera.** Sometimes you will need to hold the camera. Sometimes you will use a tripod. Whichever you do, you will need to keep the camera steady. If you are holding the camera, this will require practice and getting comfortable with the camera itself. Holding the camera with your elbows against your ribs is one technique for keeping the camera steady. Another is to put your elbows on a stable surface like a table. A tripod solves the problem of making sure the camera is steady, but it also immobilizes the camera so that it can be used in only one spot – or it can be moved along with the tripod.

• **Camera angles and shots.** Try to get a variety of angles and shots whenever you use your video camera. Used judiciously, different types of shots will make the story more interesting for the viewer. (Check out this page on MediaCollege.com http://www.mediacollege.com/video/shots/ for examples of the different types of shots you can use.) Resist turning the camera so that the picture is angled. This is disorienting for the viewer and quickly becomes irritating, and you are likely to lose viewers if you do this without good reason.

Watch this video on TV news scripting by Prof. Mark Harmon and his class. The video demonstrates the various kinds of scripts and how they are built. The video is at http://youtu.be/cQWke4zxv3w.

The best way to learn any of this, of course, is to go out and do it. Cover stories, shoot action, interview people. Carry your camera and be ready to use it. As a video journalist, you should follow two basic rules:

• **Shoot a lot.** Get different kinds of shots. Follow the 10-second rule of turning the camera on 10 seconds before you ask the first question and leaving it running for 10 seconds after you finish. (You'll find you need this space when you edit your video.)

• **Carry a pen and notebook.** Don't depend on your memory. Write things down, particularly names and titles of people. Take notes during interviews or during shooting if your camera is on a tripod.

The video interview

Reporting is about talking to people.

It doesn't matter if you are working for print, the web or broadcast. You have to know how to speak to people, ask them the right questions and get the information that you need. Here we talk about some of the specifics related to video interviewing.

• **Talk to the right person(s).** The right person is the one who has the information that you need for the story. The right person is also the one who is available and who is willing to be on camera. The right person is the one who can speak articulately and can answer questions in a straightforward manner.

• **Get a good setting for the interview.** Many factors come into play here. You don't necessarily want a scene background or the scene of the action. Remember that for the interview, you want viewers to concentrate on the questions and answers. Consequently, a noisy or busy background – one where people are going back and forth – can be distracting or can simply overwhelm the interview. One famous example of this was when Sarah Palin, then governor of Alaska and former vice presidential candidate, returned to her home state after the 2008 election. At Thanksgiving she was interviewed by a television reporter at a turkey farm. In the background, a workman was killing a turkey as Palin was answering questions. That interview was shown again and again, not because of what she said but because of what was going on behind her. (You can see the Palin interview on YouTube at this link: http://www.youtube.com/watch?v=nJd_vm9VhpU .)

• **Ask the right questions in the right way.** The questions you ask of an interviewee should be the ones that solicit the information you want. You want to conduct the interview as efficiently as possibly because you don't want to have to wade through a lot of unnecessary video during the editing process. So, have the questions you want to ask in mind before you ask them. Better yet, write them down. The questions should be short and to the point. Don't ramble and don't explain. Ask the question and stop talking. And don't interrupt. Let the interviewer speak and be ready with another question, if necessary, when the interviewee stops talking.

• **Keep it simple.** Don't repeat questions unless there is a reason to do so. Let the interviewee speak, but when you are finished with the questions and the answers, shut the camera off. You may want to get shots from a few more angles, but once you have done that, you should leave. You still have editing to do.

Video interview example

Editing the video

Video stories are imagined in a newsroom and shot on location.

But they are made in the editing process.

Video editing not long ago required lots of equipment, technical expertise, time and practice. Editing for video journalism was particularly demanding because of the deadlines imposed by news programs. Video editing required a specialist who could work quickly.

Such specialization and experience is no longer necessary. While video editing may seem technically daunting, video journalists have developed many techniques and practices that make it straightforward and well within the reach of any journalist.

And the hardware and software have changed to such an extent that video editing – while still not "easy" – is not nearly the task that it used to be.

But the hardest part of video editing was not what the videographer did but what the video journalist still does: zero in on the story idea.

Every story should have a simple, central idea that can be stated clearly. If you have that, then you can apply journalistic practices and techniques to make that story come to life. The presence of a single, well-formed story idea allows you to tell the story in a brief, simple manner, which is a requirement for good video journalism.

A number of principles govern the practice of editing video for journalism:

• Choose accuracy over everything else. Video journalists are journalists, and their primary mission is to present accurate information to viewers. Nothing should get in the way of that.

• Clarity and simplicity are the marks of good video journalism. Viewers should know what the story is about from the very beginning. They should be able to follow it logically through its presentation. One scene, cut or sequence should follow logically from another.

• The more thought, planning and work that goes into the writing and shooting of a story, the less editing will be necessary. If you sit down to edit with no plan in mind – just lots of "great" video – you are likely to be at it for a long, long time. And then, what you produce is not likely to be very good.

• Write the story – or at least begin with an outline of what you think the story will be. Know what shots you will need. Get those shots. (Be ready if something unusual happens.) And when you get to the editing part, follow the plan.

• Video editing, even with good planning, can be time consuming. Learn the techniques for making it more efficient. Most video journalists do many of the same things again and again. They don't try to be creative with the techniques. Rather they try to be creative with the content they present.

So, what are the techniques?

Storyboards. One of the time-tested tools for putting together a video story is the story board. The storyboard is a series of boxes that show different parts of a story. It can be as formal or informal as the journalist wants. It allows the video journalist to picture the story in its entirety. The words written beside the box may include the script for the story or just a phrase or two with an indicator of how much time that piece of the story takes.

Avoid repetition. Using the same shot more than once is the mark of an amateur.

Simplify transitions. Editing software gives you a wide variety of transitions to use between shots. They may look cool to the editor, but they are distracting to the viewer and they take away from the information you are trying to present. Select the simplest transitions and use them unless compelled to do otherwise.

Cutaways. Cutaways are shots that relate to the main video but not necessarily of the main event. For instance, a person giving a talk is the main video. A cutaway would be of someone in the audience listening to that person. Cutaways are used for variety – to break up the main video and prevent it from becoming boring. Plan to get cutaways when you are shooting.

Establishing shots. Get shots that give a full picture of where the event is occurring, and work those into your story in a logical way. Using a storyboard helps this process.

Pacing. The concept of pacing means present shots in a sequence that is interesting for the viewer. One of the assumptions of pacing is that no single shot or angle should stay on for too long. How long is too long? That, of course, depends on the story. There is no general rule of thumb for how long a single shot can be before it should be reviewed to see if it is seems too long. Tight editing using a variety of short scenes and shots is better than one longer sequence where the scene and angle do not change. But the video journalist must develop a good "feel" for the three kinds of movement:

- movement of characters or items within the frame or the scene
- camera movement
- movement between shots

Sound. Always check the sound to make sure that it is high quality. This part of editing is where most beginners forget and fail.

Video editing tips

- *Where possible, open with natural sound*
- *Use natural sound breaks*
- *Audio can carry from one shot to another*
- *Build sequences*
- *Establishing (wide or long) shot doesn't have to be first in sequence*
- *Use natural wipes*
- *Use in-frame motion*
- *Avoid wide shot to wide shot cuts*
- *Respect the 180-degree line /'nose point'*
- *Write to video via "writing to corners of screen"*
- *Avoid motion-to-motion edits (pan to zoom, zoom to zoom)*
- *Cover jump cuts with a good reversal or good cover video*

Mark Harmon

Video tutorials

Here are links to videos tutorials:

Mark Johnson, Shooting Video (Digital Literacy series)

http://youtu.be/JoAVYMiTGgo

Video 101: Shooting Basics (Vimeo)

https://vimeo.com/videoschool/lesson/24/video-101-shooting-basics

Video 101: Editing Basics (Vimeo)

https://vimeo.com/videoschool/lesson/24/video-101-shooting-basics

TV Interviewing Techniques
By Mark Harmon, University of Tennessee

A good interview combines several talents: research, curiosity, listening, versatility, and even a bit of bravery. Interviewing is a good skill in many professions, especially in television journalism. Of course, interviews occur in different settings and with different purposes. You may be demonstrating your poise and qualifications in a job interview. You may be gathering information by phone or in person. You may be conducting a live news interview, or hosting an interview segment to inform or entertain an audience.

Let's say you are conducting a live news interview segment. Here are some steps to follow in good interviewing:

1) Conduct research about your guest and your guest's area of expertise. This research should lead to a good set of questions. Be certain your questions cover the material well; try to ask open-ended questions. Closed questions are those that can be answered yes or no. Open-ended questions demand longer answers. This is especially critical during interviews with children. Ask a child a yes/no question and nearly always you will get a yes/no answer. Reluctant or nervous guests also may reply in yes/no terms.

2) Instruct the guest to relax and to treat the situation as a conversation. You may want to use some conversational ice breakers before the tape rolls. Also, instruct the guest to talk to you not the cameras. Few things are more distracting to an audience than a guest who does not know where to look. In the same regard, you should focus your eye contact on the guest--only turning to the camera for the opening and closing.

3) Introduce yourself, guest, and topic at the start of the segment. You may wish to begin with some background questions that help put the guest at ease. Listen closely to your guest's answers. The answers may suggest a new avenue for exploration. Don't be afraid to deviate from your prepared questions to ask follow-ups. Obviously, you should not ask a prepared question if it has been answered in an earlier reply.

4) Give non-verbal assurances to your guest. This may include normal facial expressions, eye contact, and nodding. Nodding should not be done during controversial statements or statements of opinion because it may imply agreement. Avoid "uh-huh" and "um" and other verbal assurances. These can be distracting, especially on radio but also on television.

5) If you have a "bomb," a tough or challenging question that you believe may surprise or annoy the guest, you should reserve it to near the end of the interview. Dropping the bomb too early may lead to distrust or the guest walking away. Give yourself time to establish rapport, drop the bomb, and give yourself a bit of time to recover.

6) If during the interview a guest ducks a question, you may want to rephrase and try again. It's okay to say something like "So what is the answer; will you support the bill?" After a couple tries and it becomes clear the guest won't answer, move on. Some politicians are particularly adept at the duck. Interrupt most interviews sparingly, but don't hesitate if a guest is "filibustering," talking around and through a tough question, burying it in a barely relevant sea of words.

7) Don't let a guest "turn" the interview. If a guest says, "Well, what would you do under those circumstances?" treat it as a rhetorical question and hope the guest continues to speak. If not, turn the question back, "It was your tough choice. What was your thinking?"

Circumstances clearly dictate variations in the previously-mentioned tips. A press conference may allow you only one or two questions; make sure they're good ones. An interview "grabbed on the street" may mean only one or two questions as well. Try to avoid the vacuous "How do you feel?" question put to victims of tragedy. It's bad grammar (I feel and you feel with fingers). More importantly, this intrusion on grief rarely yields good information.

Some aspects of interviewing are universal: listen, maintain eye contact, give non-verbal assurances of attention, research, and be prepared to follow promising new information.

Video to watch

Take a look at the video on Literary Journalism – an interview with UT professor Paul Ashdown located here: https://vimeo.com/10548874.

Watch this video not only for the content -- it's about literary journalism -- but also for the way it was put together. Note the following:

• *the **reporter does not appear** and is not heard at all*

• *in editing the video, the reporter has used **the cropping function** to make it appear that the subject was shot at different angles*

• *it is only after the third minute that the **point of view** actually changes*

• *the reporter uses **text to supplement and emphasize** what the subject is saying*

• *the **focus remains on the subject and what he is talking about** while some visual variety is introduced to make the video interesting for the viewer*

• *the subject **never looks directly into the camera** and is **never centered** in the frame*

4. Exercises and assignments

This chapter offers teachers and students some ways to put the principles and concepts of this book into practice.

4.1 Audio slideshow assignment

Great Smoky Mountain National Park

This assignment asks students to take the first steps in creating an audio slide show by selecting pictures and writing a script. How far they should take this after that (recording the sound, putting the slides into a slide show program, etc.) is up to the instructor.

Pictures for this assignment can be found in Google's Picasa web photo site. The pictures were taken by Jim Stovall and may be used for any classroom-related assignment. There are 33 pictures in the album.

Students do not have to use all of the pictures, but I tell my students that they should use at least 10 pictures and that the slide show should be from two to three minutes long.

The students can write their scripts using the following information, which has been taken verbatim from the Great Smoky Mountain National Park web site. (Instructors should caution students not to copy the information here; it was written for a web site, not for a slide show.)

Before starting this assignment, students should read the article on JPROF on putting together audio slide shows. < http://www.jprof.com/onlinejn/audioslideshows.html >

The pictures for this assignment can be found at:

https://picasaweb.google.com/100214416071609068916/Smokies .

Great Smoky Mountains National Park

Between 8-10 million people visit Great Smoky Mountains National Park each year, making it the most visited national park in the country.

A Wondrous Diversity of Life

Ridge upon ridge of endless forest straddles the border between North Carolina and Tennessee in Great Smoky Mountains National Park. World renowned for the diversity of its plant and animal life, the beauty of its ancient mountains, and the quality of its remnants of Southern Appalachian mountain culture, this is America's most visited national park.

From black bears to salamanders. Old-growth forests to spring wildflowers. Log cabins to grist mills. Great Smoky Mountains National Park offers a myriad of opportunities for exploring and discovering both the natural and cultural history of these ancient mountains.

Things to Do

Great Smoky Mountains National Park is a hiker's paradise with over 800 miles of maintained trails ranging from short leg-stretchers to strenuous treks that may require backcountry camping. But hiking is not the only reason for visiting the Smokies. Car camping, fishing, picnicking, wildlife viewing and auto touring are popular activities.

Most visitors come to the Smokies hoping to see a bear. Some 1,600 bears live in the park. From the big animals like bears, deer, and elk, down to microscopic organisms, the Smokies have the most biological diversity of any area in the world's temperate zone. The park is a sanctuary for a magnificent array of animal and plant life, all of which is protected for future generations to enjoy.

Seventy eight historic structures, including grist mills, churches, schools, barns, and the homes of early settlers, preserve Southern Appalachian mountain heritage in the park.

Seasons

Winter is a fickle season in the Smokies. Days can be sunny with high temperatures of 65° Fahrenheit or snowy with highs in the 20s. In the lower elevations, snows of one inch or more occur rather infrequently—usually only a few times each winter. Typically this snow melts within a few hours of falling.

Hikers enjoy the Smoky Mountains during all months of the year with every season offering is own special rewards. During winter, the absence of deciduous leaves opens new vistas along trails and reveals stone mills, chimneys, foundations, and other reminders of past residents. Spring provides a weekly parade of wildflowers and flowering trees. In summer, walkers can seek out cool retreats among the spruce-fir forests and balds or follow splashy mountain streams to roaring falls and cascades. Autumn hikers have crisp, dry air to sharpen their senses and a varied palette of fall colors to enjoy.

Nature

The wispy, smoke-like fog that hangs over the Smoky Mountains comes from rain and evaporation from trees. On the high peaks of the Smokies, an average of 85 inches of rain falls each year, qualifying these upper elevation areas as temperate rain forests.

There are at least 30 different species of salamanders in Great Smoky Mountains National Park. This gives the Smokies the distinction of having the most diverse salamander population anywhere in the world and has earned the park the nickname "Salamander Capital of the World."

Some 100 species of native trees find homes in the Smokies, more than in any other North American national park. Almost 95% of the park is forested, and about 25% of that area is old-growth forest–one of the largest blocks of deciduous, temperate, old-growth forest remaining in North America. Over 1,400 additional flowering plant species, and at least 4,000 species of non-flowering plants have been identified in the park. The park is the center of diversity for lungless salamanders and is home to more than 200 species of birds, 66 types of mammals, 50 native fish species, 39 varieties of reptiles, and 43 species of amphibians. Mollusks, millipedes, and mushrooms reach record diversity here.

History

People have occupied these mountains since prehistoric times, but it was not until the 20th century that human activities began to profoundly affect the natural course of events here.

When the first white settlers reached the Great Smoky Mountains in the late 1700s they found themselves in the land of the Cherokee Indians. The tribe, one of the most culturally advanced on the continent, had permanent towns, cultivated croplands, sophisticated political systems, and extensive networks of trails. Most of the Cherokee were forcibly removed in the 1830s to Oklahoma in a tragic episode known as the "Trail of Tears. The few who remained are the ancestors of the Cherokees living near the park today.

Life for the early European settlers was primitive, but by the 1900s there was little difference between the mountain people and their contemporaries living in rural areas beyond the mountains. Earlier settlers had lived off the land by hunting the wildlife, utilizing the timber for buildings and fences, growing food, and pasturing livestock in the clearings. As the decades passed, many areas that had once been forest became fields and pastures. People farmed, attended church, hauled their grain to the mill, and maintained community ties in a typically rural fashion.

The Great Smoky Mountains are among the oldest mountains in the world, formed perhaps 200-300 million years ago. They are unique in their northeast to southwest orientation, which allowed species to migrate along their slopes during climatic changes such as the last ice age, 10,000 years ago. In fact, the glaciers of the last ice age affected the Smoky Mountains without invading them. During that time, glaciers scoured much of North America but did not quite reach as far south as the Smokies. Consequently, these mountains became a refuge for many species of plants and animals that were disrupted from their northern homes. The Smokies have been relatively undisturbed by glaciers or ocean inundation for over a million years, allowing species eons to diversify.

4.2 Writing a VO (voice over) story for video

A 30-second video is available for viewing or download for each of the following sets of information. You can find it at the web addresses within each set. Write a VO story to go with each set based on the information provided. Your instructor may also want you to record your story and put it together with the video.

Tree cutting

• Major windstorm last week; damage heaviest in east end of town

• Rains accompanied storm added to damage; power out for several thousands homes for nearly 24 hours

• Rainy and cold every day since then

• Today, for first time since storm, crews out cleaning up some of the damage and cutting fallen and damaged trees

• Ron Yancey, president of B & B Tree Service, tells reporter that the damage last week was worst in ten years

• Yancey says damaged trees are dangerous and should be taken care of as soon as possible; estimates his crew has two weeks of solid work ahead of them

Video file download: http://bit.ly/wfmm8-ex-8-5

New roundabout

• Intersection of Dugg Gap Road and Wary Lane

• New roundabout constructed by county

• Cost: $20,000; money came from county road funds and federal grant money

• Construction underway for three months; delayed by series of heavy rains last month

• Construction completed today; opening ceremony on Saturday

• County road commissioner Sara Jess Thornburgh says roundabouts are generally less expensive than traffic lights and safer than four-way stops

• This is the third roundabout the county has built in the last two years; Thornburgh says others are being considered

Video file download: http://bit.ly/wfmm8-ex-8-6

Books win award

• Three books: *Sherman's March in Myth and Memory; The Mosby Myth: Confederate Hero in Life and Legend; The Myth of Nathan Bedford Forrest*

• Co-authored by Ed Caudill and Paul Ashdown, journalism professors at Harbrace University

• Books published over last ten years

• Books look at legends surrounding three Civil War personalities and what people think of them now: John Singleton Mosby, William T. Sherman, Nathan Bedford Forrest

• Books awarded the Phantom Grace Award for Civil War Literature; award announcement made today by the Phantom Grace Society in Philadelphia, Pennsylvania

• Award carried $20,000 prize

• Ashdown and Caudill will be on station's local public affairs show Datelines and Bylines on Sunday discussing their books

Video file download: http://bit.ly/wfmm8-ex-8-7

4.3 Facts for a story: Fuel efficiency

Write a news story based on the facts below. Follow the directions of your instructor for what kind of story you should write:

To be clear, the information below is not real.

• State Senator Michael Grady introduced a bill this morning requiring all cars built in your state to be more fuel efficient

• This is the first time efficiency standards have been challenged at the state level

• This applies to all cars manufactured in your state and raises the standard to 35 mile per gallon for most cars and light trucks

• The bill has been co-sponsored by Senators Hiram Johnson and Rutherford Hayes

• The governor of your state has not said whether he will support the bill or not

• Quote the governor of your state: "I obviously cannot not support or oppose a bill I have not received, let alone read."

• Quote Grady: "We tried to work with business and have them regulate themselves, but they just aren't doing it. We need to start getting serious about protecting our environment. We also need to be serious about not being energy dependent. The only way to do this is by using less oil. This bill gives business ten years to adapt to the changes and it provides incentives for companies to get this done early."

• Quote General Motors President Joe Rosen: "This bill would cripple our industry. It is just that simple. If this bill passes, the American auto industry might not be able to survive. We would at least have to layoff thousands of employees. The auto industry, as a whole, has been taking aggressive strides to help the environment. General Motors has been very successful in its hybrid division, and we expect to continue down that path in upcoming years."

• Quote Greenpeace Director Sarah Thomas: "This is one of the best and most progressive bills I have ever seen. It is what we need to start doing. America needs to start using less fuel. America is only 5% of the world's population, but we use 65% of the oil."

• Quote State Senator Bob Brady: "Creating a state-level fuel efficiency standard that is tougher than the federal standard is not going to save their environment, it is just going to send companies packing. Why would a company like Volkswagen stay in Tennessee and be forced to hit 35, when they could go to Alabama and just have to worry about the federal standard? The bill simply doesn't make sense."

• According to the website of the State Automotive Manufacturers Association, about 48,000 state residents are employed in automotive manufacturing.

Assignment by Nicholas Geidner

4.4 Research-based ideas for college campus reporting: 10 potential stories

By John Wihbey

Joan Schorenstein Center on the Press, Politics and Public Policy

(used by permission)

As journalism students look for deeper approaches to reporting on their campuses, they might consider the world of academic research, which can provide both fresh ideas and important perspectives. Sometimes studies are used directly by journalists in their stories; in other cases, they're a way for reporters to educate themselves about issues and to locate and tap into networks of experts.

The habit of doing a "literature review" on issues is an increasingly important skill, but it takes time to master. The ability to do a successful literature review requires knowing which **Error! Hyperlink reference not valid.** and the basics of how to read statistics; learning how to do this on deadline can give journalists an important competitive advantage in the information and media marketplace.

Below are 10 studies that can help facilitate deeper campus stories as well as enable journalists to practice engaging with primary research literature. If the full study is not immediately available online, ask a librarian for help with access and get familiar with your institution's available databases. Also be sure to look at the citations in studies, as they will provide a road map to other important research in the field. To the extent you can, ask university officials for school-wide background data to help support your story and localize a given issue.

Finally, remember that this is just a representative batch of studies. Whether you're writing about tuition increases, sexual assault policy, binge drinking, Greek life or flu outbreaks, there's a wealth of deeper research just waiting for you at places such as Google Scholar and PubMed.

1.   **Multitasking and learning: A 2012 study published in Computers & Education,** "No A 4 U: The Relationship between

Multitasking and Academic Performance," examines how the use of Facebook — and engagement in other forms of digital activity — while trying to complete schoolwork was related to college students' grade point averages. Is multitasking prevalent around your campus? Do students see downsides or upsides? How much do they reflect on their own study habits and use of time? How do faculty members feel about its role in the classroom?

2.   **Jobs and their effects:** Many researchers have studied the negative relationship between student work — both on and off campus — and the typical effects on learning. However, student work may have some under-appreciated, positive effects. A 2012 study in the Journal of College Student Development, "The Effects of Work on Leadership Development Among First-Year College Students," looks at the lives of students earning their way through school. What percentage of students on your campus has jobs? How do they perceive the tension between work and learning? Do they believe there are hidden benefits?

3.   **Diversity experiences:** A 2011 study in the Review of Educational Research, "Promoting Participation in a Diverse Democracy: A Meta-Analysis of College Diversity Experiences and Civic Engagement," examines earlier research to understand the relationship between diversity experiences and civic engagement in later life. The study provides insights into the kinds of diversity experiences that have the most meaningful impact in terms of lifetime development. How does your campus do on these issues? What is the breakdown between structured and unstructured diversity experiences, as the study defines them?

4.   **Student debt:** How students feel about rising debt levels has been a significant media topic in recent years. But how do students on campus feel that it's influencing choices of majors and classes — and career choices? Two studies can help inform this reporting: a 2012 study from Harvard University and the University of Virginia, "Student Loans: Do College Students Borrow Too Much — or Not Enough?"; and a 2011 study from the University of California-Berkeley and Princeton University, "Constrained After College: Student Loans and Early-Career Occupational Choices."

5.   **Exam habits:** Students have many time-honored techniques for studying, but some methods are much more effective than others, according to the latest research. A 2012 study published in Psychological Science in the Public Interest, "Improving Students' Learning With Effective Learning Techniques: Promising Directions

from Cognitive and Educational Psychology," rated the utility of 10 specific methods based on cognitive and educational psychology research. How do students on your campus study for exams? Who taught them the techniques they use — high school teachers, peers, parents? Is the campus faculty doing enough to teach effective learning?

6.   **Research and online skills:** A 2012 report from Project Information Literacy, "Learning Curve: How College Graduates Solve Information Problems Once They Join the Workplace," seeks to better understand the needs of professional employers and the research skills and habits young people use on the job. The study finds that students often lack certain skills, and rely too much on the Internet. How do students on your campus find information? What do the faculty and librarians think about the information-seeking skills of the students they see? Is your institution doing enough to prepare students for the needs of the workplace in an information-based economy?

7.   **LGBT student views:** A 2012 study published in the Journal of School Violence, "The Effect of Negative School Climate on Academic Outcomes for LGBT Youth and the Role of In-School Supports," analyzes survey data relating to a sample of 5,730 LGBT students between the ages of 13 and 21 who had attended secondary schools in the United States. How do LGBT students compare their high school and college experiences? How do the academic climates compare? How do LGBT students feel their secondary school experiences inform their current lives and views?

8.   **Women and campus politics:** According to survey data, American women consistently score lower on questions of political knowledge than do men. This difference makes women less likely to vote, run for office or communicate with their elected representatives. A study published in the journal Political Behavior, "Gender Differences in Political Knowledge: Distinguishing Characteristics-Based and Returns-Based Differences," analyzes data in the United States from 1992 to 2004 to try to isolate the underlying causes of this male-female split. How are women faring in campus politics and student government? Are there enough outlets for political discussion? How many women would consider running for political office? How many female majors are there in the political science and government departments? Is the campus doing enough to educate and encourage women leaders?

9.   **Rural and non-rural students:** One often-hidden dimension

of campus diversity is the rural/urban/suburban split among students. A 2012 study from the University of North Carolina at Chapel Hill, "Rural-Nonrural Disparities in Postsecondary Educational Attainment Revisited," examined data on approximately 9,000 students and found some notable differences. How comfortable do students from rural backgrounds feel on your campus? What has their experience been like and how do they believe it is different? Do they feel sufficiently supported?

10.   **Taking time off:** A 2010 study published in the American Educational Research Journal, "Male and Female Pathways through Four-Year Colleges: Disruption and Sex Stratification in Higher Education," tracked academic performance, financial aid support, prior high school experiences and life choices to determine why students choose nontraditional education pathways. How many students take semesters off? Why do they do this? Do they see drawbacks or benefits? Is there a gender, socio-economic or racial dimension evident in the patterns on your campus?

- See more at:
http://journalistsresource.org/skills/reporting/research-based-ideas-college-campus-reporting-10-potential-stories#sthash.3cLu2FND.dpuf

4.5 Building a story with public data

Read through the following summary and be prepared to discuss with you class how you would build a story using the data presented in these links.

Student Loans: Do College Students Borrow Too Much — or Not Enough?

As the United States struggles to recover from the Great Recession of 2007-09, many would-be students remain optimistic about their professional futures. < http://pewresearch.org/pubs/2191/young-adults-workers-labor-market-pay-careers-advancement-recession > Some question the wisdom of assuming substantial debt to earn a college degree, however, especially when jobs for young people remain relatively scarce. As of 2012, the average debt load was $25,000 for a graduating senior, < http://www.projectonstudentdebt.org/state_by_state-data.php > with a median figure of about $13,000. < http://libertystreeteconomics.newyorkfed.org/2012/03/grading-student-loans.html > But high school graduates earn about $20,000 less than college graduates in terms of median annual income, according to Census figures.

A 2012 study from Harvard University and the University of Virginia published in the Journal of Economic Perspectives, "Student Loans: Do College Students Borrow Too Much — or Not Enough?" examined data on student loans in the United States, including broad trends in borrowing over time and optimal loan amounts based on course of study and institution.

Key study findings include:

• On average, college education increases total life earnings: In 2012 figures, "the college graduate would have compiled a total of approximately $1.2 million in earnings net of tuition at age 64 as opposed to approximately $780,000 in total earnings for the high school graduate." This gap was approximately $200,000 from 1965-85 but steadily increased by 1985 to the current gap of more than $400,000.

• For the average student, a standard ratio of 8-10% loan burden to average post-graduation income has remained relatively stable: "To put this in perspective, an individual with $20,000 in student loans could expect a monthly payment of about $212, assuming a ten-year repayment period. In order for this payment to accrue to 10 percent of income, the student would need an annual income of about $25,456, which is certainly within the range of expected early-career wages for college graduates."

• "Students who have chosen a technical field — in the broad categories of computer science, engineering, and math — tend to earn more than the average and more than those with education or humanities undergraduate concentrations."

• As of November 2011, the "unemployment rate for college graduates (including those with advanced degrees) was 4.4%, while high school graduates faced an unemployment rate of 8.5% and those with collegiate attainment less than a B.A. faced an unemployment rate of 7.6%."

• The percentage of undergraduates taking out any type of debt for school has grown in the last 20 years, from 19% in 1989-90 to 35% in 2007-08. Over the period 1960-80, the U.S. government distributed more grant money than loans; after 1980, loans steadily increased while grants stagnated until a recent — and significant — increase in 2009.

• Private-sector borrowing to finance higher education has increased significantly in recent years: "Private sector loans were about $1.5 billion (constant 2009 dollars) in 1995-96 [and] grew to $21.8 billion by 2007-08, representing about 20% of all loan funds."

The researchers note that while most students will see a high return on their investment in college, incurring debt "is also a lottery with significant probabilities of both larger positive, and smaller or even negative, returns." They advise students to carefully consider borrowing limits by evaluating how previous students on a similar path have fared economically and professionally.

In related research, a 2012 Federal Reserve Bank of New York study notes that "about one-quarter of borrowers owe more than $28,000; about 10 percent of borrowers owe more than $54,000. The proportion of borrowers who owe more than $100,000 is 3.1 percent, and 0.45 percent of borrowers, or 167,000 people, owe more than $200,000."

4.6 Video interview

Review the video interview section in Chapters 3 of this book, particularly the section on the video interview. After you have done this, take a look at the following video interview: http://www.jem230.com/lecture-notes/13-video-journalism-2/

Watch this video not only for the content -- it's about literary journalism -- but also for the way it was put together. Note the following:

- the **reporter does not appear** and is not heard at all

- in editing the video, the reporter has used **the cropping function** to make it appear that the subject was shot at different angles

- it is only after the third minute that the **point of view** actually changes

- the reporter uses **text to supplement and emphasize** what the subject is saying

- the **focus remains on the subject and what he is talking about** while some visual variety is introduced to make the video interesting for the viewer

- the subject **never looks directly into the camera** and **is never centered** in the frame

Now that you have done that, your assignment is to produce a two- to four-minute video based on a short interview with a relative or friend who remembers the assassination of John F. Kennedy in 1963. The video you produce should be modeled after those on this page and should contain the following:

- Title slide

- Video that includes: clips with different croppings or viewpoints; transitions, such as a cross-dissolve; identifier

- Credit slide that includes your name as the producer and the date the interview was conducted.

A still picture insert is not required but would certainly enhance the video.

Post the video onto YouTube or Vimeo and sent the link to the instructor by the deadline the instructor has designated. Make sure the video is public, not private.

Here are some videos of students who have completed this assignment:

http://www.youtube.com/watch?v=S0mj4rOaGbg

https://vimeo.com/54343000

http://www.youtube.com/watch?v=atcmEa7xRqY&feature=youtu.be

https://www.youtube.com/watch?v=x5kKanwPTF4

4.7 Scavenger Hunt: Sources

You and one teammate have --- (amount of time given to you by the instructor) to find quotes to fit the categories listed below. You must go out and find people who fit for each topic. Do NOT use best friends, roommates, boy/girlfriends, etc. as sources. All quotes must be from people you talk to in person. Teammates must stay together during the whole exercise (no dividing and conquering). A source can only be used for one category (no double dipping). Instructors may adjust these assignments with regard to local issues and news.

• Student journalist on a recent issue in journalism.

• A professor on a piece of current research.

• Business owner near campus about crime on or near campus.

• Lifetime local resident on recent local issue in the news.

• A student-athlete on the pressures of being an athlete.

• Sorority member on the benefits of being in a sorority.

• A female independent on the benefits of not being in a sorority.

• Freshman student on the first week of classes and academic standards.

• Senior student on the increasing costs of a college education and balancing class with part or full-time jobs.

• SUBMISSION: For each quote you must provide the source's full name, year in school if a student or title or profession if non-student, and e-mail address.

Assignment written by Amber Roessner

4.8 Sex Offenders Registry

This is a multi-platform story, which means you need text (300-400 words), 60-90 second video, headline and two-sentence web summary, links to appropriate web sites (at least two). Append a list of sources that you used, including telephone numbers and emails.

1. Go to the state sex offenders registry. You may access the data a number of ways, not all of which are very useful. You want to select by geography, which may be a certain city and street, a zip code, or proximity to a certain address.

2. Put in your local address. Then request the listing of offenders within a few blocks. If nothing turns up, make the search area larger. You may even look to see which ones live in the same apartment complex as you.

ALTERNATIVE: If you are home for the weekend, try your hometown address. Or you may search from your local workplace.

3. After you have the list, look at the sorts of offenses for which they were convicted.

4. INTERVIEW: You will conduct an interview with at least two people in the area that you searched. DO NOT INTERVIEW

ROOMATES OR FRIENDS. That is because they do not take you seriously and usually make poor interview subjects. You will need to take notes for the text story and record video of the interview for the video story. DO NOT INTERVIEW A SEX OFFENDER.

Things to ask or consider, to ask in your interview:

1. Are you aware of this database?

If yes, have you ever used it? When and where? Did you take any action as a result of what you found out?

2. (If the interviewee is proximate to offenders) Will this information cause you to take any action, such as being more cautious or even moving?

3. Ethical questions to consider, perhaps to ask of interviewees: Should a person be on this list forever, say someone who committed an offense 10 years ago and has a clean record since then? Should a journalist be dredging up these old offenses, which many people would have forgotten and could impede rehabilitation efforts by compromising employment prospects for the offender?

Should a similar database exist for all convicted felons? Why or why not?

Assignment written by Ed Caudill

4.9 Beginning-of-the-term audio slideshow

Welcome back for the new semester. And now it's time for -- headaches with getting into required classes at the last minute; lines at a bursar's office to pay those fines for parking and overdue library books; those same lines for finding out where your scholarship or loan money went; finding a parking place; overpriced textbooks at the bookstore. But there may be some fun stuff, such as events sponsored by the university (especially in fall semester, when the freshmen are getting to know their way around), and sports events. You need a two- to three-minute slide show on your topic. Remember, it's for a general university audience, so you need to provide details.

1. It should contain 20-30 pictures with shots that are long range, medium range and close-up.

2. Record audio narration to go with the slides. This is where you'll provide details of the event.

3. Have a title card, which is a full-page graphic.

These are the minimum requirements. The slide show may also contain voices of sources, ambient sounds, and music. You may use text cards that add to the narration.

You may use any software or hardware for the project. In JEM 200, you were introduced to Audacity software for audio editing and Picasa software for putting the pictures together with the sound. Picasa is a free program from Google that comes in PC and MAC versions. Other useful software include iMovie or a PC equivalent, or Final Cut Pro.

Here is a short article on JPROF about audio slideshows:
http://jprof.com/onlinejn/7steps-audioslideshow.html

Assignment written by Ed Caudill

4.10 Scavenger Hunt: Public records

You and up to two teammates have until --- to find the following information. You can use any means at your disposal (except stealing from other groups) to find the information. The information must come from reliable sources. Teammates must stay together during the whole exercise (no dividing and conquering).

1) What was the United Way of America's total revenue for 2005?

2) What was the unemployment rate for the state in May 2011?

3) What was the official undergraduate enrollment of the University of – (your major state university) for the fall semester 2011?

4) Who is the sponsor of the Recalcitrant Cancer Research Act of 2012 (H.R. 733)?

5) In 2011, what percent of your state's population is Hispanic or of Latino origin?

6) How many aggravated assaults occurred on the major state university campus in your state in 2009?

7) How many people entered the Great Smoky Mountains National Park in February 2010?

For each item above, provide your answer in a full sentence following AP style (e.g., According to _____, the second item on the Knox County Commissioners agenda was _____). Below the sentence, provide the full link to the place you found the data or provide the name, title and contact information for your source.

For each completed quote, the team will be given -2, 1 or 2 points. You get 1 point for submitting a correct answer. You get 2 points for a submitting correct answer from an acceptable/publishable source. You will lose 2 points for any answer you get wrong.

SUMBISSION: You must come back to the classroom and submit your answers by --- . Your answers must be typed. Please let me know what category each quote is being submitted for.

Assignment written by Nicholas Geidner.

4.11 Scavenger Hunt: Photos

You and up to two teammates have until --- to find and take and submit the following photos. The photos cannot be staged. Teammates must stay together during the whole exercise (no dividing and conquering).

1) Photo of someone studying in the library.

2) Photo of someone making food.

3) A portrait of a professor in his or her office.

4) A wide-medium-tight sequence of an iconic part of campus.

5) A wide-medium-tight sequence of an intersection near campus.

6) A 3-image action sequence (can be any repeated action).

7) A wide-shot of an empty room on campus.

8) Photo of a campus employee working outside.

9) Photo of a campus sport logo.

10) Photo of a political sign (e.g., yard sign, window sign, button, etc.)

For each item above, provide a caption in a full sentence following AP style (e.g., John Doe, second-year in communication studies, eats lunch in the University Center Tuesday.).

For each completed photo, the team will be given 1 or 2 points. You get 1 point for submitting a photo. You will get 2 points for submitting a photo that could be published. You will lose 1 point if your caption is incorrect. You will get a 1-point bonus for completing each of the photo sequences.

SUMBISSION: You will submit your photos via Twitter. Please include the following hashtag on all submissions: #-----------.

Assignment written by Nicholas Geidner.

5. The First Amendment

The First Amendment to the U.S. Constitution protects five important freedoms: religion, speech, press, assembly and petition. Even though the First Amendment has been in the Constitution for almost the entire history of the republic, the idea of its protective powers has been slow to develop.

5.1 Religion

Many Americans have their history wrong. They believe that the first European settlers of this nation came to America because they believed in the right to practice religion and worship freely.

Actually, many of them came because they wanted to practice their religion freely. They did not care about the right of people outside their own groups to observe a different set of beliefs.

During the colonial years there was a much religious intolerance and state supported religion practice as there was in England or any place else in Europe.

But that began to change in the late 18th century, particularly through the writing and efforts of Thomas Jefferson, who challenged the government's role in religious observance.

Freedom of religion today

Today, through many events and court cases, we have developed some fundamental understandings about what the words of the First Amendment mean (sometimes referred to as the 'establishment clause'):

Individuals have the right to believe, practice religion, and worship as they see fit.

Individuals are not required to support any religion or religious organization.

The government cannot establish or support any religious organization.

The government must remain neutral in dealing with religious organizations and beliefs.

Even with these fundamental understandings, there are still many controversies and issues surrounding the First Amendment's guarantee of freedom of religion and of the state neutrality toward religion. For instance, consider these:

– prayer in schools

– creationism

– posting the Ten Commandments in government buildings

– requiring the recitation of the Pledge of Allegiance in schools

– blue laws

– putting Christmas decorations on public property

The list could go on.

5.2 Speech

If the First Amendment means anything, we believe, it means that we have the right to speak our minds — to say what we think, right?

That's correct.

But it wasn't always so.

In the early days of the republic, laws were passed that protected the president and administration from criticism.

Many states had laws restricting the freedom of speech, especially in the South where is was against the law to advocate abolition (freeing slaves). Yet Americans have always enjoyed debating the issues of the day. They like to argue, disagree, and even diss one another. From colonial days Americans have sought solutions to social, economic and political problems by vigorous and animated discussion. Sometimes those discussions have turned violent. More often than not, however, the discussions have ultimately resulted in commonly agreed upon solutions and principles.

Despite its halting beginning, "free speech" proved its value more than once, and the concept is now deeply embedded in the American psyche.

Still, as much as we honor free speech, we are sometimes not very careful in preserving it. Our tendency to censor speech that is disturbing or disagreeable -- or that doesn't agree with what seems to be the majority opinion -- sometimes gets the best of us. We also have a tendency to think that if we limit speech in certain ways and on certain topics, we can solve some pressing social problem. Particularly during national crises, we tend to believe that if we can just stop people from saying certain things, our nation will be more secure.

When we do this, however, we are defying our own best instincts and a logic that experience teaches again and again. We can never successfully keep people from saying what they believe in, from believing whatever they choose, and from expressing those beliefs publicly. Other societies try doing this, and eventually they explode.

People do not like to be told that they cannot say something.

Neither do we.

Our job as Americans is to protect free speech wherever it is threatened. We should constantly be on guard against the thinking that restricting speech will somehow make us a better society. We should preserve our unique place in the world as a society who values its individual citizens and protects them even when they say or do things that are not popular.

5.3 Press

This part of the First Amendment

> *'. . . or of the press . . .'*

has generated a great deal of debate and much litigation throughout the history of the republic.

Just what did the founders of the Republic mean by that? How have we interpreted that phrase since it was originally written?

Answers to those questions have filled many volumes, but generally we believe that the government should not censor printed material; that it should not exercise prior restraint (preventing something from being printed or distributed) on publications; and that it should not hinder the distribution of printed material.

In journalism, this freedom extends to the practice of journalism itself. Reporters should be able to gather information. Government bodies – courts, legislative units, boards, etc. – should operate in the open. Government records should be available to all citizens who request them. In some cases, reporters are protected from disclosing their sources because of this clause in the First Amendment.

Two important areas where the freedom to publish is limited are: libel or defamation; and copyright and trademark.

Libel or defamation

Libel – the concept that words can harm a person's reputation – is an ancient principle of common law. A person's reputation has value, and when that value is diminished, a person can see redress from the courts.

Yet there is the First Amendment, which says society has value in being able to speak freely. How do we resolve this conflict?

Despite the language of the First Amendment, libel laws exist and are, occasionally, enforced. Journalists must be careful about libel.

Modern defamation laws say that to win a libel case, you must prove

- publication (more than just two people have to see/hear it)

- identification (can the person defamed be identified)

- defamation (did the words have potential to do real damage)

- fault (was there negligence or some mitigation)

harm (is there provable damage)

Defenses against defamation

Statute and case law provide some strong defenses for people facing libel actions:

- truth – powerful defense (society values truth)

- qualified privilege – is the situation one that relieves people of libel responsibility? Reporters depend on the concept of qualified privilege to report public affairs. For instance, they may report the arrest of a person who is ultimately is declared innocent of a crime.

- absolute privilege – Some instances, such as a legislator speaking in a meeting of the legislature, can say anything he or she wishes without regard to libel laws.

- statute of limitations – Courts do not like old cases, particularly in civil matters. Many states have a statue of limitations provision that says a libel suit must be filed within two years of the alleged libel.

- Constitutional privilege – This privilege protects news media from suits by public officials and public figures. It comes from a 1964 decision, New York Times v Sullivan. The results of this case make virtually impossible for any well known figure to recover damages in a libel action.

Still, the threat of the costs of litigation are real, and journalists should be careful to avoid them if possible.

Copyright
The freedom to write and publish is not unlimited.

One area in which that freedom is limited is that of copyright and trademarks, which are part of a larger area of law known as intellectual property. People who create what we might term generally as "intellectual property" – books, musical works, art, sculpture, articles, poems, etc. – have some protection in the way that those works are used by others. If you draw a picture or write a poem, that picture or poem is yours (at least for a limited amount of time), and no one else can reprint it without your permission.

There are things that copyright does not cover, however.

Facts cannot be copyrighted. Let's say you are the only writer covering your high school basketball game, and you write a story about it for the high school paper. Another publication can take the facts that you have described – the details of the game, the score, etc. – and use them in its description of the game.

That publication, however, cannot use your account of the game. The expression of facts can be copyrighted, but the facts themselves cannot.

Like facts, ideas cannot be copyrighted, but the expression of those ideas can. For instance, you can paint a picture of a tree, and that painting will be copyrighted. Someone else can paint a picture of the same tree. That's ok, as long as they do not use your painting.

The protection of a copyright is limited in two important ways. One is that it does not last forever. Currently, copyrights last for the life of the creator, plus 70 years. If the copyright is owned by a corporation, the copyright lasts longer. A copyright does not last forever. At some point, all creative works become part of the "public domain"; that is, everyone owns them. Consequently, the works of William Shakespeare, for instance, are in the public domain, and Shakespeare can be quoted at length without anyone's permission.

The second limitation of copyright is through the concept of fair use. This concept has been developed to encourage the dissemination of ideas and information without either putting a great burden on the user or infringing on the rights of the creator of the work. Fair use means that in certain limited circumstances, a copyrighted work – or more likely, some portion of it – may be used without the permission of the holder of the copyright.

Courts have looked at four things in considering what is fair use:

– the nature of the copyrighted material – how much effort it took to produce it;

– the nature of the use – for instance, material used in an educational setting for educational purposes is more likely to be thought of as fair use;

– the extent of the use – how much of the copyrighted material is used, just a few words or a whole passage;

– commercial infringement – most importantly, how much does the use hurt the commercial value of the work.

Unless material is being used in a very limited way, you should always get permission to use copyrighted material. Holders of copyright can be very aggressive about enforcing their copyrights, and the unauthorized user of a copyright can be fined substantially. Many people in education believe that they can use any material in any way they wish, and it will be considered fair use. That is not the case. Educators are bound by copyright laws as much as anyone else.

Note: Material on the Internet has as much copyright protection as anything else. Some people believe that whatever is on a web site is in the public domain, and that is not the case. Just because material is easy to access does not mean that it does not have copyright protection.

Trademark

A special protection for the commercial use of words, phrases and symbols is trademark.

Many companies go to great lengths to protect their trademarks because that is how the public identifies their products. What if, for example, a shoe company named Nuke started using the Nike symbol, the swoosh, on its shoes? Consumers might become confused about what product to buy, and Nike, which holds a trademark on the swoosh, might be hurt by that.

5.4 Assembly

The First Amendment guarantees that people can get together – peaceably – and talk about whatever they want to discuss.

Courts have almost always recognized that governments have the power to regulate time and place of assembly when the public's safety and convenience is an issue.

But governments are prevented from saying to a group of people that they cannot meet when the reason for their meeting is legal.

According to the First Amendment Center:

First Amendment freedoms ring hollow if government officials can repress expression that they fear will create a disturbance or offend. Unless there is real danger of imminent harm, assembly rights must be respected.

About the picture:

Before 1920, most women in the United States could not vote. In the 19th century, they had few legal rights at all, and the social customs against women being seen in public unless they were with another woman or accompanied by a man were strict and unacceptable by today's standards. When women starting petitioning for the right to vote in the early part of the 20th century, they began holding parades, exercising their right to assembly. Here is the beginning of the Washington Suffrage Parade of 1913, a significant event in the history of the suffrage movement. For more information on this parade and its effect on the eventual passage of the Nineteenth Amendment, go to Seeing Suffrage.

5.5 Petition

When an individual

- calls the tax assessor's office to complain that property taxes have gone up too much,

- attends a town meeting public officials and policies are questioned,

- joins a legal street demonstration to gain publicity for their cause,

- pays a lobbyist or joins a group that pays someone to go to Washington or the state capital to argue for a cause,

then that person is petitioning 'the Government for a redress of grievances' – a right protected by the First Amendment.

The right to petition the government was very much on the minds of the Founding Fathers. As colonists, they had asked King George III and the government in London many times to pay attention to what they wanted. Mostly, the people in England ignored them.

So, when it came time to write the Declaration of Independence, they included the following in their reasons for declaring independence:

In every state of these Oppressions We have Petitioned for Redress in the most humble terms: Our repeated Petitions have been answered only by repeated injury.

Governments in the U.S. do not have to agree with the petitioner or do what he or she asks. But they must listen.

And they cannot retaliate against the petitioner for asking.

Compared to the other parts of the First Amendment, the right to petition the government has not generated much litigation or attention among scholars over the years. Perhaps, according to Adam Newton, writing for the First Amendment Center, that is because it continues to work so well. The petition clause is the tacit assumption in constitutional analysis, the primordial right from which other expressive freedoms arise. Why speak, why publish, why assemble against the government at all if such complaints will only be silenced?

About the picture:

Mary Gertrude Fendall (left) and Mary Dubrow (right) standing outside what is likely National Woman's Party headquarters, holding between them a large sign containing text of a Resolution Addressed to Senator Edward J. Gay with a long unrolled sheet of paper, presumably signatures on a petition, laying on the ground in front of them. The sign was in support of the Nineteenth Amendment, which would given women the right to vote. The sign mentions mentions that "President Woodrow Wilson has urged the passage of the Federal Suffrage amendment before the Senate of the United States and again recently before the whole Congress of the United States as a necessary War and Reconstruction Measure . . ." Wilson first publicly declared his support for the amendment on Jan. 9, 1918. He asked the Senate to pass the amendment as a war measure on Sept. 30, 1918. The amendment was passed in the House on May 21, 1919, and in the Senate on June 4, 1919. Library of Congress photos, circa 1918-1919.

5.6 History

First Amendment Videos

Gitlow v. New York

Videos of Dr. Dwight Teeter discussing various aspects of the First Amendment and how it developed can be found at these links:

https://vimeo.com/9852487

https://vimeo.com/9754284

https://vimeo.com/9748541

https://vimeo.com/9823451

https://vimeo.com/9772215

The First Amendment grew our of four concepts of behavior of human beings in society (as identified by Teeter, Le Duc, and Loving):

• marketplace of ideas

- individual fulfillment

- safety valve

- self-governance

Each of the concepts is important for an understanding of why people in the 18th century -- the time when America earned its independence from Great Britain and adopted the Constitution -- believed in the notion of freedom of speech.

The marketplace of ideas is based on the concept that no one person or entity knows the truth that can be applied to every action of mankind. Since no human has the authority to say what is right or wrong or true or not true, ideas must be expressed and tested. The famous English author John Milton gave voice to the marketplace of ideas (although he did not use that term), and many in the 18th century followed his line of thinking. Simply put, the concept is that if everyone can express his or her ideas, the truth will eventually emerge.

Individual fulfillment means that all people have potential to become more than they area. As humans, they need the freedom to express themselves and to try to expand and improve their character and productivity. By doing this, they are of benefit to the entire society. People can define themselves through their individual expressions.

The idea of freedom of speech as a safety valve means that individuals can express opposition to authority without punishment, and this -- in the long run -- has a calming effect on the political society. If people know that at the very least they can speak and be heard, they are less likely to rebel against the whole structure of the state.

Finally, free speech is the basis of self governance. No society can claim to have its people self governing if it does not allow free expression of ideas.

These ideas were floating around and much debate when America won its independence from Great Britain in the 1780s. A great deal of free speech had already been practiced by the Founding Fathers as they were making war against Britain and as they were setting up their own government, so individual rights did not seem like a critical issue.

But as Americans debated the ratification of a new Constitution in 1787 and 1788, many prominent people -- people such as Patrick Henry and Samuel Adams -- opposed the Constitution because they believed that it would concentrate too much power in the hands of two few people. Individual liberties -- the right to speak and to assemble, for instance -- would be threatened by the newly powerful centralized authorities.

To counter those arguments, proponents of the Constitution promised that, once the document was ratified and put into place, they would support a set of amendments that would guarantee the rights about which the opponents were concerned. James Madison, who had been a chief architect of the Constitution itself, took the lead in drafting these amendments, which eventually became known as the Bill of Rights.

The First Amendment is the first of 10 of these amendments. Some deal with individual liberties. Others deal with how the government much handle individuals accused of a crime. Still others restrict government action in certain areas.

The First Amendment is not first because the Founding Fathers considered it the most important one. The historical record indicates that they clearly did not. Still, the fact that it is first has invested it with much value. What is means exactly is still a matter of vigorous debate.

The politics of the First Amendment

The First Amendment, as Professor Teeter says in the video in the previous section, is "the chance product of political expediency." (He's quoting Leonard Levy, another First Amendment scholar.) How did that happen?

James Madison was the chief author of the new Constitution that had been put forth by those wanting to form a strong central government in 1787. As such, Madison became one of the leaders in arguing for its ratification. The Constitution was the product of weeks of delicate compromise on many of its points, and Madison feared that any changes to it would destroy its chance for passage.

That's exactly what the opponents of the Constitution hoped, and they began complaining that the Constitution did not protect individuals from the powers of government to take away civil liberties, such as freedom of speech, freedom of the press and the right to trial by jury. This debate took place in just about every state that considered the Constitution but it was conducted fiercely in Virginia, Madison's home state. Opponents were led by Patrick Henry, the popular orator of the Revolution and a man still active in politics. Henry and other feared a powerful central government.

Sitting on the fence in this debate were the Virginia Baptists and other religious groups who had been fighting against the established and official religion of the Anglican church. Baptists were persuaded by these argument -- especially by the lack of separation of church and state.

This put them and James Madison in an awkward position. Madison and the Baptists had been strong allies in the fight against an established church. Now, Madison appeared to be abandoning that principle with his support for this new Constitution.

In truth, Madison did not think that these rights needed to be protected by the new Constitution, and he feared that adding them would upset the fine balance he had struck to complete the Constitution to begin with. But recognized and understood the concerns of his friends, the Baptists. He also knew that without their support, it would be unlikely that Virginia would ratify the Constitution. And if Virginia, the largest state among the original 13 colonies, did not do so, the Constitution itself would not be ratified.

So, Madison promised to support a bill of rights that would be added to the Constitution after it had been ratified and the first government had been established. He promised to run for Congress and then to do what he could to introduce the necessary amendments. That stance put Madison in the position of admitting that there was something lacking about the Constitution that he so ardently supported. Still, he did want was necessary and was able to persuade the Baptists and other concerned religious groups to his side.

The Constitution was ultimately ratified, and the new government was put in place.

Madison was elected to the Congress but initially found little support among his colleagues for immediately amending the Constitution before it had had a chance to work. Still, he had made a promise, and he used his massive intellect and political skill to keep that promise

As historian Forrest Church has written:

His (Madison's) authorship of the First Amendment constitutes perhaps his most abiding legacy. Acting on the crucial impetus provided by his Baptist constituents, he etched church-state separate and freedom of conscience into the American code.

For more on the ratification battles over the U.S. Constitution, see the Teaching American History website.

The First Amendment in the 19th and early 20th centuries

By the early 1790s, the First Amendment, along with the other nine amendments that constituted the Bill of Rights, had been ratified -- and seemingly quickly forgotten. During the single term of the John Adams presidency (1797 - 1800), Congress passed and the president signed the Alien and Sedition Acts that outlawed criticism of the president and those in power. (Figure -.-)

Republicans such as Thomas Jefferson and James Madison -- in opposition to the Federalists -- could do little about these acts. The Supreme Court had not yet established itself as the body that could review laws passed by Congress for their constitutionality, so there was at that point no check on congressional power. The acts themselves were ineffective in stifling criticism of the president, and fortunately, they expired after two years. By that time, Thomas Jefferson had been elected president, and the Federalists would never return to power. The Alien and Sedition Acts stained the Adams presidency, and they made heroes out of those they meant to persecute.

The First Amendment and the other parts of the Bill of Rights were meant to restrain Congress. People of the early republic saw their power and intent as limited. States and state constitutions were still the source of governmental power that Americans recognized as most important. Recall that the First Amendment begins with the words: "Congress shall make no law . . ." This phrase was deliberate and taken seriously by the people of the time. Congress could not make laws, but states certainly could.

In addition, we need to understand that the greatest concern of those who composed the First Amendment was religious liberty and the free exercise of religious practices -- not free expression. Madison, Jefferson and their allies wanted to prevent the new government from establishing an official church -- not guaranteeing free speech or a free press. They wanted to build a "wall of separation" between the government and the church.

In this, they were highly successful. Religious liberty and the free exercise of religion -- without interference from the government became an established principle of the nation. It is one that remains in effect today, so much so that we often take it for granted.

But the idea of freedom of expression had a tougher time.

The chief and abiding political and moral issue facing American in the first half of the 19th century was slavery. Slave had been in America for 300 years by that time, and slavery had worked its way into the social, political and economic system. As tobacco and cotton -- particularly cotton -- grew in importance, slavery as a means of producing these products also strengthened.

The emotional and political costs were enormous.

Whites, especially those in the South where slavery existed and grew, lived in constant fear that slaves would one day rise up in bloody revolt. Those fears were not groundless. Slaves in the newly formed nation of Haiti had done just that, and every Southern plantation resident had nightmares that the same thing would happen on their land, even though they might fool themselves into thinking that their slaves were happy and contented.

Northerners shared many of those fears, and because their economic systems did not depend so much of cotton and tobacco, Northern states were able to free themselves slowly from the slavery system. Still, the fear of the possibility of a slave revolt was national.

Consequently, those who advocated freedom for slaves -- emancipationists and abolitionists -- were not welcome in many places. Southern states passed laws against the printing and distribution of abolitionist newspapers. They also outlawed the open advocacy of emancipation or abolition. In some cases, newspaper editors who wrote about such things had their presses destroyed, were run out of town, or in a few tragic instances killed. Clearly, these situations offend our 21st century ideas of what the First Amendment should mean, but most people of the time did not view the First Amendment in this fashion.

One man who did was a Kentucky newspaper editor named Cassius Marcellus Clay. Clay had come from a slave-holding family in Kentucky but during his college days at Yale had been persuaded that slavery was wrong. He became an emancipationist, someone who advocated the gradual freeing of slaves. (Abolitionists favored immediate freedom for slaves.) Clay was stubborn and tough. He was criticized harshly for his stance and physically attacked several times for what he wrote about slavery.

Clay was one of the few men of the 19th century to say that the First Amendment to the Constitution should protect people like him from any government intrusion.

The nation did not hear or heed Clay, and those who advocated unpopular ideas were subjected to legal and extra-legal pressures to conform or remain silent. During the Civil War, Lincoln and his administration brought government power to bear against those they felt were endangering the war efforts.

The one bright spot in the 19th century for civil liberties came in 1868 when the nation ratified the 14th Amendment, which said that states could not deprive people of liberty or proper without resorting to "due process of law" and could not deny people the "equal protection" of the law. This amendment was put in place to assure that freed slaves would be given their full rights in states where slavery has previously be prevalent. This was clearly a check on state power and an assertion that the U.S. Constitution was the ultimate law of the land. It was another 50 years before this idea -- that states had to be subject to the will of the federal constitution -- took hold in any meaningful sense. When it did, in a 1925 Supreme Court ruling, it changed the entire balance of legal power in the United States and set us on the road to our modern thinking about First Amendment protections.

Meanwhile, America endured several national crises, including what was then known as the Great War (1914 - 1918). We call it World War I today. It was a time, more than any other in the nation's history, when the American government, under the direction of Woodrow Wilson, strayed from the principle of protecting free expression.

In 1917, the year America entered the war, Congress passed the Espionage Act which made it a crime "to willfully cause or attempt to cause insubordination, disloyalty, mutiny, or refusal of duty, in the military or naval forces of the United States," or to "willfully obstruct the recruiting or enlistment service of the United States."

The next year saw passage of the Sedition Act, which outlawed spoken or printed criticism of the U.S. government, the Constitution or the flag.

The Wilson administration was vigorous in using these laws and other means to suppress dissent. Part of the woman suffrage movement -- the Woman Political Party led by Alice Paul -- were particularly irritating to the administration. Despite America's entry into the war, members of the NWP continued to picket the White House, demanding that Wilson support suffrage at home while he was touting the expansion of democracy abroad.

The women picketers were arrested for "obstructing sidewalk traffic" and hauled off to jail. At first, their sentences were relatively light (two to six days in many cases), and the administration hoped the arrests would discourage future demonstrations. The opposite occurred.

Women continued to picket the White House, and the signs they carried grew more pointed. When they were rearrested, they were given longer sentences. The women asked to be treated as political prisoners, a status they were denied. They then we on hunger strikes. Prison officials, with the administration's approval, subjected the women the women to forced feeding, a torture process that kept the women alive but weakened and injured them.

Once out of jail, the suffragists continued to picket the White House and tell the story of what happened to them at the hands of government officials -- all for non-violently demanding their political rights. The picketing and protests continued after the war and up until the passage of the 19th Amendment that gave women the right to vote.

The treatment the suffragists received was not as harsh that meted out to those charged and convicted under the Espionage and Sedition Acts. Some people spend years in prison for the crime of protesting the nation's involvement in the Great War -- violating the rights to speech and petition that the First Amendment was supposed to protect.

Courts were of little use in protecting these rights. The Supreme Court on numerous occasions had the opportunity to check the administration's actions but failed to do so.

As America came out of the war, many people were disturbed by the heavy-handedness of the Wilson administration in suppressing dissent. They believed that America was in danger of losing its way as the beacon of free societies and that more attention should be paid to actively protecting civil liberties than to simply saying that "Congress shall make no law . . ."

This change in attitude did not occur all at once. Rather, it was a step-by-step process that began with the Supreme Court ruling in Gitlow v. New York in 1925. In that decision, for the first time, the Court said that because of the 14th Amendment, Constitutional protections, such as those in the First Amendment, applied to state actions. This decision opened the door for a wide variety of other decisions during the next 40 years that strengthened protections guaranteed by the Bill of Rights.

30052633R00090

Printed in Great
Britain
by Amazon